£3.50

Who are the poor?

JOHN S. POBEE

Who are the poor?

The Beatitudes as a call to community

THE RISK BOOK SERIES

WCC Publications, Geneva

Cover design: Rob Lucas

ISBN 2-8254-0884-0

© 1987 WCC Publications, World Council of Churches,
150 route de Ferney, 1211 Geneva 20, Switzerland

No. 32 in the Risk book series

Printed in Switzerland

Table of contents

Preface

Some time ago, the Ecumenical Institute at Bossey and the World Council's Programme on Theological Education co-sponsored a seminar on "Ministry with the Poor". It fell to my lot to give five Bible studies at that seminar.

The seminar was attended by participants from Africa, Asia, Europe, Latin America, New Zealand and the USA. Some of them were rich, some not-so-rich. The experience of addressing such a mixed group was as exhilarating as it was painful. For it held up the mirror to me and I began to see more clearly my blind spots and privileges. One has come to appreciate more acutely that as an academic one has been enjoying a privileged position and can never be a down-and-out poor, at least materially. So in these reflections I have no desire to speak for the poor; nor do I seek to be my brother's or sister's keeper, an expression which has paternalistic undertones. Rather, I want to be my brother's brother or sister's brother, to be in solidarity with the poor so as to bring fellow human beings to a sense of community and to an authentic sense of responsibility for the less fortunate.

In recent years much has been said on this topic. Notable is the great insight of liberation theology that God is on the side of the oppressed. It emphasizes that the preferential option for the poor is a key, if not *the* key to the understanding of the gospel. In the wake of this insight it has become fashionable to use the rhetoric of the preferential option for the poor, sometimes with little commitment to it. But the subject is too vital for it to be left to such rhetoric. We need to go back constantly to the Bible, and to our own specific contexts of affluence and poverty.

John S. Pobee

1. Introduction

"Blessed are you who are poor, for yours is the kingdom of God" (Luke 6:20). In the Gospel according to Matthew there is a parallel text which reads: "Blessed are the poor in spirit; for theirs is the kingdom of heaven" (Matt. 5:3). Whichever of the two texts is the original, the words form part of what are known as the beatitudes.

The beatitudes take their name from the recurring word *beatus* in the Latin text. *Beatus* translates the Greek word *makarios*, often rendered in English as "blessed" or "happy".

In whatever language they are read, the beatitudes cannot fail to impress the reader with their poetry, characterized as they are by rhyme, rhythm, word play and parallelism. Parallelism is a common feature of Hebrew poetry. A good and familiar example is Psalm 8:4:

> What is man that you are mindful of him,
> the son of man that you care for him?

The two parts of the verse are two ways of stating the same point but with emphasis. Parellelism is a balanced structure between two halves of a line or verse or even between verses. There are, of course, different types of parallelism. The parallelism of the beatitudes is what is known as synthetic parallelism. The second line of each beatitude contains the blessing which completes the pronouncement and promise. Thus, for example, "theirs is the kingdom" is the content of the blessedness pronounced on the poor.

As the text of the beatitudes stands in Matthew, the poem consists of two stanzas: Matthew 5:3-6 and Matthew 5:7-10. The blessedness relating to the poor, those who mourn, the meek, the hungry constitute one stanza, and those relating to the merciful, the pure in heart, the peace-makers and the persecuted constitute the other stanza.

It is perhaps not without significance that Jesus taught in a poetic form. Some scholars like B.F. Easton have argued that Jesus used the poetic form because he required his disciples to memorize his teaching. This would be on the example of the rabbis who encouraged their disciples to memorize their teachings. It is, however, difficult to prove this to have been the intention of Jesus. What can be asserted is that poetry undoubtedly has practical value in the sense that it aided interpretation.

Jesus sought to challenge his audiences with the word of God and to confront them with the demands of the gospel.

Biblical scholars have reached the consensus that the three Gospels, Mark, Matthew and Luke, were written from the same standpoint. They are remarkably similar, at several points following the same order of events and using identical language, even if at certain points they are dissimilar. The majority of New Testament scholars are of the opinion that Mark's Gospel was the first to be written and that Matthew and Luke made use of it in composing their respective accounts. They are convinced that at least for Matthew, Mark's Gospel is the basic text on which he built. On that basis the Sermon on the Mount is inserted after Mark 3:19, i.e. the call of the twelve who had accepted Jesus' gospel and are willing to follow him. And so it is argued that in the Sermon on the Mount Jesus sets forth how those who claim to be under the gracious rule of God order their lives.

We have of course been addressing the text as it is found in Matthew. This is for the simple reason that the text in Matthew is the most familiar to believers, especially through the liturgy of the churches. However, that should not make us lose sight of the fact that there are striking differences between Luke and Matthew with regard to the beatitudes.

First, the difference in the text itself. While in Luke we read: "Blessed are you who are poor, for yours is the kingdom of God" (Luke 6:20), Matthew has "Blessed are the poor in spirit, for theirs is the kingdom of heaven" (Matt. 5:3). We shall pick up this in Chapter 2.

Second, in Matthew the beatitudes belong to the Sermon on the Mount, while in Luke they are a part of the sermon on the plain (Matt. 5:1 cf. Luke 6:17). Third, in Matthew the beatitudes are followed by an analysis of the human personality which is sacred at all points and is to be reverenced and cultivated. On the other hand, in Luke the beatitudes are followed by a section on loving and doing good to fellow human beings (Luke 6:27-45). This, in modern terms, may be taken as a warning against activism in the name of religion, when it is not rooted in a Christ-centred life. In other words, in a truly Christian context, social engagement and involvement should be rooted and anchored in a devotion to Christ the Lord. The

Czech theologian Jan Milic Lochman expresses this point in some quaint words in his book *Reconciliation and Liberation*: [1] "This many-sided salvation is not floating, unmoored, homeless and nameless blessing. They (New Testament writers) do not leave vague and undefined the basis of this reality of salvation (*soteria*) and of our knowledge of it. Salvation... means the person, the history and the name of Jesus Christ. It is to be understood in the light of this specific centre."

The importance of tying in social action and Christology cannot be overstated. It is crucially important for the Christian to let his/her engagement in social action be rooted in a clear understanding of the person of Jesus Christ in whom his/her faith is grounded.

Fourth, there are fewer beatitudes in Luke than in Matthew:

Matthew	*Luke*
1. Blessed are the poor in spirit; for theirs is the kingdom of heaven, 5:3	Blessed are you who are poor, for yours is the kingdom of God, 6:20
2. Blessed are they who mourn; they shall be comforted, cf. Isaiah 61:2-3	Blessed are you who weep now; for you will laugh, 6:21b
3. Blessed are the gentle; they shall inherit the earth, 5:5	—
4. Blessed are they who hunger and thirst after righteousness; they shall be satisfied, 5:6	Blessed are you who hunger now; for you will be satisfied, 6:21a
5. Blessed are the merciful; they shall obtain mercy, 5:7	—
6. Blessed are the pure in heart; they shall see God, 5:8	—
7. Blessed are the peacemakers; they shall be called children of God, 5:9	—
8. Blessed are they who are persecuted for righteousness' sake; theirs is the kingdom of heaven, 5:10	—
9. Blessed are you when they slander and persecute you and falsely accuse you of every wrong because of me. Be glad... because in heaven your reward is rich, 5:11-12	Blessed are you when people hate you and exclude you and denounce and defame your name as wicked on account of the Son of Man, 6:22

[1] Belfast, Christian Journals Ltd., 1980, p.46.

4

What is laid out above hardly needs comment. Instead of eight or nine beatitudes as in Matthew, there are four in Luke. As Luce sums up the difference between Matthew and Luke in his commentary, *The Gospel According to St Luke*,[2] "Matthew calls 'blessed' those who possess certain *moral* and *spiritual* qualities: Luke refers to those who are enduring *physical* hardship and suffering. But if the circumstances be kept in mind under which the words were originally spoken, the differences will be seen to be not fundamental. Jesus was speaking to the disciples, not to the crowds; that is to say, to those who had already shown some readiness to receive his teaching."

Fifth, Luke has what are known as the woes, i.e. harsh warnings against the wealthy (Luke 2:24), those who are filled now (Luke 6:25a), those who laugh now (Luke 6:25b). Those woes concern those who fail to be committed to the kingdom (Luke 6:24-26).

For our purposes it is not necessary here to draw out the significance of these differences except that they are evidences of the editorial responsibility of the evangelist. Indeed, the very fact that in Matthew the beatitudes form part of the Sermon on the Mount is yet another evidence of the editorial responsibility and style of the Gospel writer.

Theologians have drawn attention to the fact that the Sermon on the Mount is a composite work, giving a general summary of Jesus' teaching. It is neither a discourse nor a system of ethics; rather, it is a declaration of the will of God with respect to certain matters. It is a symbol of the Christian way of living and a quarry for Christian services. Its general theme is the achievement of character or moral personality through reverencing it in others and through merging one's interests with those of the community. As holy writ comments: "Those who lose their lives shall save it" (Mark 8:35, Matt. 16:25; Luke 9:24). The theme of the Sermon on the Mount is the grace of God and of the gospel; it warns against projecting religion in terms of legalism and self-sufficiency. It is in this context that the beatitudes are set.

---

[2] Cambridge, Cambridge University Press, 1933, pp.144-145.

Scholars are divided in their attitude to the Sermon. There are three major attitudes. For one group of theologians, the Sermon represents "perfectionist legalism", i.e. it is concerned with the absolute demand of God on believers and every bit of it is demanding. A second group of scholars reads the Sermon as "impossible ideal", i.e. they demand the impossible so that people may be thrown more on the mercy of God, once they realize their impotence to be good in their own right. According to a third group of scholars, the Sermon is an "interim ethic", i.e. it was not meant to be the moral structure to be followed by the disciples for all time; rather it was designed to face the people with a last opportunity for heroic effort in the crisis situation which called for decision either for God or against God.

Since there is more than one way of looking at life, I am prepared to concede that there is some truth in each of these theories about the Sermon. But it can at the end of the day be read as the charter of the kingdom (cf. Matt. 4:23). In a sense they are expatiations of the covenant law reinforced with a new urgency. The Sermon on the Mount is a declaration of the will of God with respect to certain matters.

Earlier on the point was made that the theme of the Sermon on the Mount is the grace of the gospel. The word *makarios*, translated "blessed", picks up this theme of grace. The blessing is conferred by God alone upon persons with a certain character. *Makarios* is a predicate and the nature of the blessing is defined in the second part of each beatitude. In the light of this, the word "happy" is not a good translation for *makarios*, for it does not exactly capture the fact that blessedness partakes or should partake of the character of God and that it is on a high moral and spiritual level. It is this fact that makes the theme of blessedness sound rather strange at face value. It is odd to think there should be "happiness" when one is persecuted. Here is no preaching of sadism, or masochism. Here is no Stoic acceptance of untoward circumstances. According to the Stoics, a philosophical school which included a person like Seneca, it was a sign of virtue to show fortitude and accept misfortune. Thus Stoics were exhorted to show joy in the face of outrage, to bear pain with loftiness of spirit and to be thankful for suffering.

The beatitudes are not promoting that kind of Stoic teaching. In the case of the Stoics it was a matter of accepting fate, what is fixed. Contrary to that, in the teaching of Jesus there is no inflexible logic. Indeed, the course of the world rests in the hands of a personal God from whom everything comes and to whose glory everything is. God is in control of the situation. Further, the message is that to live the beatitudes is to reflect the divine image which alone brings about inner calm and serenity and salvation. No wonder the faithful are invited to be as perfect as their heavenly Father (Matt. 5:48). Blessedness comes from sharing God's life. There is also a contrast between the happiness that comes from finding the things of life that really matter, such as humility, goodness, purity, etc., on the one hand, and the happiness which in the popular mind comes from pleasure and prosperity.

As to the content of the blessedness we are lucky that the beatitudes had Old Testament and Jewish antecedents and parallels. Commentators have drawn the following parallels and antecedents:

Blessed are the poor (cf. Ps. 34:6 and Prov. 19:17)
Blessed are the mourners (cf. Isa. 57:18; 61:1ff.).
Blessed are the gentle/meek (Ps. 37:11)
Blessed are those who hunger and thirst after righteousness (cf. Isa. 51:5,6,8)
Blessed are the pure in heart (cf. Ps. 24:4)
Blessed are the peace-makers (cf. Isa. 52:7; 57:18-21)

According to Ecclesiasticus 25:7-10: "There are nine who come to my mind as blessed, a tenth whom my tongue proclaims: the man who finds joy in his children, and he who lives to see his enemies' downfall. Happy is he who dwells with a sensible wife, and he who ploughs not like a donkey yoked with an ox. Happy is he who sins not with his tongue, and he who serves not his inferior. Happy is he who finds a friend and he who speaks to attentive ears. He who finds wisdom is great indeed but not greater than he who fears the Lord."

With such a wealth of information in the Old Testament and Apocrypha on blessedness, it is proper to seek an understanding of blessedness in the Old Testament. Perhaps the most rewarding quarry is Psalm 144: 12-15:

> Then our sons in their youth will be like well-nurtured plants,
> and our daughters will be like pillars carved to adorn a palace.
> Our barns will be filled with every kind of provision. Our sheep
> will increase by thousands, by tens of thousands in our fields.
> Our oxen will draw heavy loads. There will be no breaching of
> walls, no going into captivity, no cry of distress in our streets.
> Blessed are the people of whom this is true; blessed are the
> people whose God is the Lord. (NIB)

This text describes blessedness in a variety of ways — in biological and material terms; economic terms; political and social categories and religious/spiritual terms.

Biological and material blessedness

In the text quoted above, three examples are given of this kind of blessing. It is a blessing from God, not to be taken for granted, that one's sons grow up. In an age when we are conscious of the community of men and women and are warned again and again against sexism, one cannot fail to be struck by the fact that the psalmist seems to see blessedness in terms of the growing up of sons. This, needless to say, is evidence of the Semitic captivity of the biblical culture in which it is almost a disaster to be a woman. Was it not a prayer repeated regularly in the synagogue: "Blessed be Thou that you have made me neither a Gentile, a woman nor an ignoramus"? In the light of the full extent of the biblical teaching, one would assert that Jesus would go beyond this to see blessedness in the growth of both sons and daughters. How much I, as a son of a matrilineal African society, appreciate it! For as the Akan say, if you get a daughter, you have an inheritance, a heritage that shall never be lost. Indeed, Psalm 144 itself goes on to say it is a blessing to have beautiful daughters. Perhaps in the light of references to "vigour", we had better say it is a blessing to have a healthy family. The enjoyment of good health and wellbeing too are a blessing from God which may not be taken for granted. This is a rationale behind the engagement of churches in the society to provide wholeness to the individual, the family, the clan, the nation and humanity, in Africa as elsewhere. As Pope Pius XII puts it in his Encyclical letter *Evangelii Praecones* dated 2 June 1951: "Such outstanding works of charity are undoubtedly of the highest efficacy in preparing the souls of non-Christians and in drawing them to the faith and to the practice of Christianity; besides, our Lord said to the apostles: 'Into whatever city so ever you enter, and they receive you... heal the sick that are therein and say to them: the kingdom of God is come upon you'." [3]

Whatever else blessedness is, it is also material. That was the basis for Christian concern and protest against some Nestlé products in Africa which are believed to be injurious to lactating mothers. Though blessedness in our times often has liturgical or ecclesiastical overtones, in the Bible it is also the enjoyment of physical health and wellbeing for oneself and one's family members.

Economic blessedness

The psalmist, using the paradigm of an agrarian society, also describes blessedness in terms of successful farming, both agrarian and pastoral — good harvests of grain, increase in healthy sheep and oxen, in short, abundant harvest and healthy livestock. The psalmist's emphases in this direction are on productivity and material abundance, phrases not uncommonly heard in our contemporary discussions of development. These biblical insights regarding economic blessedness are translatable into modern terms. The search for a new and just economic international order today is a search after blessedness. It is wrong to idealize and idolize poverty. God desires wellbeing for all human beings in order that they may be able to worship the living Father who desires good things for all creation. Conditions of abject poverty such as afflict peoples all over the world, not only in Africa, Asia and Latin America, but also in parts of affluent Europe and America, are a denial of the will of the loving and sovereign Lord. Perhaps we shall do well to recall Luke 4:18: "The Spirit of the Lord is upon me, for he has anointed me to preach the gospel to the poor; he has sent me to announce release to the captives and restoration of sight to the blind, to set free the downtrodden." Need we add any further comment to this clear statement of the need for men and women of God to struggle for wholeness for humanity? This understanding of blessedness is a clear reference to productivity and material abundance as fundamental values.

---

[3] R. Hickey, *Modern Missionary Documents and Africa*, Dublin, Dominican Publications, 1982, p.92.

Political and social blessedness

Economic blessedness cannot be sharply distinguished from political and social blessedness. According to the psalmist, blessedness includes the absence of any cries of distress in our city squares. Perhaps we can visualize a village square in Africa or the agora in Athens where people come together to discuss the affairs of the village or city, to see how they can improve the circumstances of the people, the open space in the city where justice was administered and business transacted. Perhaps we can imagine a political rally at which the oppressive and aggressive policies of the government in power in Accra or Pretoria or Washington are denounced. According to the psalmist true blessedness excludes any form of oppression or captivity, be it social, sexual, racial or religious. For most people the oppressed are those who are discriminated against, brutalized, marginalized, etc. But these are only one type of captivity. Some are prisoners of hate, e.g. those so blinded by the atrocities of apartheid, racism and tribalism as to hate any person from the other group. Others are prisoners of prejudice and pride. Some are so much in captivity to their own culture that they are always puzzled by the values and actions of others without even attempting to understand them. Some are in captivity to modern technology, to punctuality, etc., etc. In our day several third-world countries are held in servitude, resulting from the exploitation of private capital as from state absolutism.

However, it is not only the marginalized who are in captivity; those who are politically and socially comfortable can also be in captivity. Too many people are in captivity to political systems and bitterness. President Reagan of the United States of America represents many in the USA who have a pathological fear of communism. In South Africa many whites are in captivity to the ideology of apartheid. Listen to the testimony of Miss Joyce Scott, a white South African Methodist woman. She once went to see the film "Cry the Beloved Country", which takes its name from the book of Alan Paton, a description of the race situation in South Africa. This was a turning point in her life. It so disturbed her that she became sensitive to the realities of the South African political and social situation. She writes: "From that day I never saw a crowd of African people without a deep chill of fear edging into my heart. It was *Die Swart Gevaar*, the fear of the 'Black danger' of which I had vaguely heard invading my own heart with deep, incalculable fear."[4]

In other words, while she enjoyed the privileges of apartheid society, she now came to realize her captivity to the ideology of apartheid and her imprisonment to a political system. She was also in that sense poor, like the African who is poor, discriminated against and imprisoned by bitterness towards the white race.

Blessedness, whatever else it may be, includes the absence of anger, despair, disillusionment and fear. It excludes doctrinaire divisions and bitterness towards peoples of other races, classes, sexes, religions, etc. which not infrequently are the driving force behind one's political ambitions. Blessedness enjoins on us the necessity to banish the enemy image so characteristic of so much of contemporary political rhetoric and practice. True blessedness means peace at home and abroad, inside us and outside us. The quest after human dignity for all peoples, all races, all sexes, for youth as for the aged, is a quest after blessedness.

Religious and spiritual blessedness

In the biblical vision of blessedness, the foregoing do not constitute the sum total of true blessedness. Material, economic, political and social wellbeing represent the horizontal or temporal dimensions of wellbeing, so to speak, and that is only part of the story. Fullness of life has horizontal as well as vertical dimensions. This latter is expressed by Psalm 144:15: "Blessed are the people who have the Lord for their God." Beyond building a new society in terms of good health, creating conditions of plenty, peace and justice, true blessedness is as well the realization of each one's potentiality as a human being. Dietrich Bonhoeffer wrote in his *Letters and Papers from Prison* that "to be a Christian does not mean to be religious in a particular way, to make something of oneself (a sinner, a penitent or a saint) on the basis of some method or other, but to be a man".[5]

---

[4] "Apartheid", in *Three Colours of Hate*, eds Barak Odhiambo, Joyce Scott and Som Dass, Nairobi, African Christian Press, 1980, p.18.
[5] London, SCM Press, 1967, p.118.

To be truly religious is to be a true human being, one bearing the image and likeness of God (Gen. 1:27). It is to experience and understand the love of God and, therefore, to seek to be in selfless and self-giving devotion to fellow human beings. Furthermore, seemingly secular pursuits are the context of spiritual salvation and blessedness (Matt. 25:31-46). Nicolai Berdyaev has articulated this point thus in his book *Origin of Russian Communism*:

> The question of bread for myself is a material question, but the question of bread for my neighbours, for everybody, is a spiritual and a religious question. Man does not live by bread alone but he does live by bread and there should be bread for all. Society should be so organized that there is bread for all, and then it is that the spiritual question will present itself before men in all its depth: It is not permissible to base a struggle for spiritual interests and for a spiritual renaissance on the fact that for a considerable part of (humankind) bread will not be guaranteed... Christians ought to be permeated with a sense of the religious importance of the elementary daily needs of people, the vast masses of people, and not to despise these needs from a sense of exalted spirituality. [6]

Spirituality is not to opt out of this world; the truly spiritual person is committed to this material world but in a healthy, caring, loving and selfless fashion. This may be termed holy materialism.

Religious and spiritual blessedness excludes unbelief. It is rooted in the faith that "unless the Lord build the house, their labour is futile who build it. Unless the Lord preserve the city, the sentry watches in vain. It is useless for you to be early in rising while being late in sitting up, eating the bread of toil; for he gives to his beloved sleep. Behold, children are a legacy from the Lord; the fruit of the womb is his reward. As arrows in the hand of a mighty man, so are the children of one's youth. Blessed is the man who has his quiver full of them. They shall not be put to shame when they speak with their enemies in the gate" (Ps. 127:1-5).

Christians begin with God and end with God. Trustful dependence on God is the remedy against corroding anxiety. And that belief in a purposeful Creator God is the basis of our

---

[6] London, Centenary Press, 1937, pp.225-226.

hope in this troublesome world. We need it to give us proper perspective and protection against hopeless distortions of horizontal dimensions of blessedness.

Belief is not enough; it is verified, among other things, in worship. Again the Psalmist says: "Blessed is everyone who reveres the Lord, who walks in his ways" (Ps. 128:1). And it is this belief that sets people free to repent of their life-long attitudes and to find forgiveness from one another and God. Religious belief bears the fruit of right conduct. And finally, religious blessedness involves looking beyond this present world to the consummation of the purpose of God which is called the kingdom of God or salvation. To that extent blessedness is more or less the same as the kingdom of God and salvation.

The biblical understanding of blessedness is comprehensive, holistic, ecumenical, incorporating many facets and excluding any heresy of sectarianism which destroys salvation. Certainly the horizontal dimension is important: bodily beauty and health are important indices of blessedness. But the vertical dimension which is the religious and spiritual dimension is an equally important index of blessedness. That vertical dimension is what "protects human freedom from our human temptation to idolatry — both our own and that of other people. It demythologizes secular (or religious) salvation and in doing so brings out its true value all the more clearly". [7]

We should never lose sight of the biblical insight that ongoing effort in the here and now is what guarantees any future.

As we have seen, in Matthew's Gospel the beatitudes belong to the Sermon on the Mount. Permit me to indulge in some speculation about the mountain. Several times in the Gospels references are made to a mountain. The temptation narratives, for example, come to their climax with Jesus on an exceedingly high mountain and tested to worship Satan who is prince of this world. Later still, the transfiguration, at which there is an experience of beatific vision, takes place on a mountain (Matt. 17:1). At some point we hear of the Mount of Olives where the painful agony in the Garden of Gethsemane is portrayed (Matt. 26:30ff.). A quick review of references to mountains leaves a

---

[7] Lochman, *op. cit.*, p.25.

twofold impression. The mountain is a place for revelation, a place to enjoy the beatific vision of God, a place of retreat where we may pray, meditate and be vouchsafed a vision of the kingly rule of God. But it is also a point of temptation to bastardize the true vision of God's rule. Let us therefore approach and ascend to the holy mountain with Jesus to experience a vision of the kingly rule of God. But let us also be warned of the danger to idolize, abuse, misuse the true vision.

To go up a mountain you need the cooperation of all organs and limbs — strong feet to climb; lungs to breathe the rarefied air; eyes to see the paths and danger spots; strong shoulders to carry your knapsack, etc. As we approach the mount of the Lord, let us bring our whole selves to him, to yield every aspect of our being to the God who awaits us there and is going ahead of us and will speak to us on the mountain as he did of old. "Come, let us climb the Lord's mountain... that He may instruct us in his ways and we may walk in his paths" (Isa. 2:3).

2. Blessed are the Poor

There is every indication in our time that the world has come of age, in the sense that even in the secular world there is a greater sensitivity to the plight of the marginalized of the world. Institutions like the United Nations Education, Scientific and Cultural Organization (UNESCO), United Nations Disaster Relief Organization (UNDRO), United Nations Children's Fund (UNICEF), Food and Agriculture Organization (FAO) are living manifestations of that sensitivity. Religious people and institutions too have been working hard at making the world sensitive to the factors that promote poverty in nations — unjust, international structures, false indices of development, political oppression, etc. The record of the World Council of Churches in this area of conscience-awakening is quite respectable.

For all that, however, the world press carries constant news of increase in the volume of refugees, of the ever-widening gap between the rich and the poor, with the latter getting poorer every day. In 1981 the World Bank reached the alarming conclusion that by the end of the decade 70 percent of the population of sub-Saharan Africa would be living in absolute poverty, a situation in which "the basic necessities of human existence are lacking". There are signs of this prophecy of doom coming true all over Africa already — Ghana, Uganda, Zaire, Sierra Leone, Burkina Faso, Liberia, etc. Worse still, Africans in the painful poverty around are showing signs of a sense of powerlessness, a sense of defeatism, a sense of betrayal — if not by God, at least by those nations of the North whom they had joined in a life and death struggle against the fascist regimes of Hitler and Mussolini. Instead of finding the freedom they sought, they are now enslaved by their very allies. In the face of the poverty, there is a deep sense of hurt on the part of Africans.

The picture painted above is true of Asia and Latin America as well; it is also true of the Pacific. The dimensions of poverty in the world today are staggering and depressing. It is in this context that the proclamation "Blessed are the poor" is made. Is this a sanctioning of poverty and therefore an invitation to leave things as they are? Does it reflect a gross insensitivity to conditions of abject poverty?

We have noted the difference between the Matthean and Lucan versions of this beatitude. While Luke has "blessed are you poor; for yours is the kingdom of God", Matthew has "blessed are the poor in spirit, for theirs is the kingdom of God".

It is easier to resolve the difference between "kingdom of God" (Luke) and "kingdom of heaven" (Matthew). They are synonymous but Matthew has a predilection for heaven, arising out of Jewish piety in which heaven is a periphrasis for the holy, ineffable God. Both phrases mean the sovereign rule of God, the situation in which the will of God is done with glad submission. As in the Lord's Prayer: "your kingdom come, your will be done on earth as in heaven" (Matt. 6:10; Luke 11:2). In the parallelism of the verse the coming of God's kingdom and doing the will of God on earth are synonymous.

In Jesus' teaching the kingdom was realized in and through his ministry, particularly his acts of power. "If I drive out demons by the Spirit of God, then the kingdom of God is come upon you" (Matt. 12:28). In his healing ministry the kingdom was made real, and those held in chains by Satan were released at his word. In a similar vain the disciples were asked and authorized to heal the sick wherever they went and to declare that "the kingdom of God is upon you" (Luke 10:8-9). But such social action is not the sum total of the kingdom. For even in the ministry of Jesus a consummation is yet to arrive. When he fed the hungry, it was only a prefiguration of the Messianic banquet of the kingdom.

There are three points to be made with regard to the kingdom. First, never once did Jesus speak of spreading or building the kingdom. This comes as a surprise because not infrequently good Christians are heard to say they are building Christian civilization in Africa and Asia. Apartheid, for example, is sometimes justified as a way of defending Christian civilization in a continent which allegedly stands in danger of stepping back into chaos, anarchy and primitivity! Unlike such positions, the kingdom, according to the Gospels, is the subject, not the object, of human activity. The kingdom comes. "May thy kingdom come" goes the prayer. We, rich or poor, theologian or lay, priest or politician, do not build it. We are either accepted into it or excluded from it (cf. the parable of the sheep and the goats). This, however, does not mean we have nothing to do. Ours it is to live the life of love, the mark of the kingdom in the here and now, and in eschatological expectancy.

Second, Jesus in the Gospels hardly ever alluded to himself in so many words as Christ or King. In fact in the Synoptic Gospels he is very reticent on this point. This is not without significance, especially if it is recalled that Jesus rejected political interpretations of Christ and kingdom. On the one hand, Jesus' challenge to injustice and its perpetrators as well as his espousal of the oppressed had clear political ramifications and overtones. But the kingdom is more than politics; it is more than human rights. It is rather an invitation to return to human dignity in Christ who was the express image of the invisible God. The kingdom has an implied ideology but is not first and foremost an ideology. This warns us against politicizing the kingdom. It warns us against confusing any social or political programme with the gospel. The kingdom, like the gospel, designates vitality.

Third, Jesus seldom spoke of God as King. God is more often than not addressed as Father. Where the kingdom image is used, it is often touched up with the Father image. Similarly, when the forensic imagery of justification is used of the salvation wrought in Christ, the reference is to the court of a father not a king or judge. Thus the gospel is against legalism. The good news of the redemption brought in Christ is an invitation to all humanity to realize themselves as members of the family of brothers and sisters in Christ, rich and poor alike.

It is more difficult to address the part of the beatitude that refers to the "poor" (Luke), for which Matthew has "the poor in spirit". It is striking that Luke's Gospel which normally has a focus on the Spirit is on this occasion silent on the Spirit. Besides, promising blessing on the poor is more difficult to understand than promising it to "the poor in spirit". New Testament scholars have a canon that the more difficult reading is the better one. Therefore, the Lucan version may be judged more original than the Matthean version. In other words, "poor in spirit" is an interpretative gloss on the original simple "poor". And so, what does "the poor" mean?

In recent years much mileage has been made of the Greek and Hebrew words translated as "poor". In this style of scholarship, one Greek word, *ptokos*, and its Hebrew equivalent, *'ani*, have been much discussed. The often heard English idealizations of "the poor" in the Bible are mainly built, rather insensitively, round *ptokos* and *'ani / 'anu*. However, as Friedrich Hauck and Ernst Bammel have demonstrated incontrovertibly in the entry on *ptokos* in the *Theological Dictionary of the New Testament*, [1] there is a considerable variety of words for "poor" in Hebrew, e.g. *dal, ebyon, rash, misken*, etc. though a smaller range in Greek. It is thus inaccurate, when reporting on biblical attitudes, to lump all together under the one English word "poor".

The word *ptokos* derives from a root *ptosso* which means to be thoroughly frightened. In popular language it came to be used of one who is dependent on others, like a beggar. Such a one has no security and is anxious over his life and future and is dependent on others. This history of it makes it possible to use the word poor of the humble children of God who are dependent on God. And this brings us to the Hebrew background.

As mentioned earlier, several words describe the poor, even if in a majority of cases i.e. about one hundred, the Hebrew is *'ani*. *Dal*, for example, describes a social class and status marked by social distress and physical weakness (Prov. 8). *Rash* has social and economic connotations, especially in Wisdom literature, and refers to the famished, the needy. The predominant *'ani* describes a relative dependency, rather than the state of social distress. Be that as it may, the whole complex of words speaks of the materially deprived and the not so well endowed. Such were represented in Israel as well as in the law and the prophets as the object of God's special care. For example, according to Proverbs 19:17, "He who is gracious to the poor is lending to the Lord; he (i.e. the Lord) will repay him for his benevolent action." Not only are the poor the special concern of God, but poverty is a sign in the world of human beings that God's purpose that they live in a community of brothers and sisters is not being fulfilled. In the brotherhood and sisterhood of the covenant, God demands a sense of community and that the poor should share in the privileges of the covenant, of the "land flowing with milk and honey". In the words of Rabbi Koehler in his book *Jewish Theology* "charity is not a gift of

---

[1] Grand Rapids, Eerdmans, 1968, Vol. VI, pp.885-915.

condescending love but a duty". [2] In other words, in the earlier years of Israel's history, the poor were seen in the context of the affirmation of the value and importance of each person.

As Israel developed, there was a corresponding development of the idea of the poor. When under King Jereboam II Israel was an economic success, there was exploitation and marginalization of the poor by the rich (cf. Amos 4, 6:1-10; Hosea 8, 10:3). Although they continued to practise religion, offering the stipulated sacrifices and keeping feast days, the rich by the exploitation of the poor had brought about the breakdown of the covenant community; individualism had taken over from a communitarian life. The eighth-century prophets strongly denounced those who pauperized their compatriots and co-religionists. Pauperizing others is a crime against human beings as well as against God who will take up their cause and stands with the poor over against those who pauperize them. As the *War Scroll* of the Qumran sect on the banks of the Dead Sea puts it: "Blessed be the Lord God of Israel... in giving vigour to the shoulders of the bowed, and... to the lowly spirits; firmness to the melting heart." [3]

In this context, the word "poor" acquired a deeper meaning. Material poverty is only one dimension of the biblical meaning of *'ani*, albeit a critical one. But the poor person came to be the faithful Israelite who relied only on the Lord, unlike the rich who relied on wealth and power over others. The poor became the typical devout Israelite in contrast to the rich degenerate Israelite. Thus *'ani* (=*ptokos*) becomes synonymous with *qadosh* (the holy one), *nasid* (the poor one), and *tsadiq* (the godly or righteous one). The word "poor" thus acquires a religious meaning and status. Material deprivation is proto-typical or paradigmatic for all kinds of deprivation, helplessness, oppression and suffering. The poor know their need and, therefore, can rely only on God.

And so according to Psalm 34:6: "The poor man called and the Lord heard and saved him out of his troubles" (see also Isa. 61:1-2). Thus spiritual poverty comes to match that of physical and material want. This is the rich background of the beatitude:

---

[2] 1918, p.487.
[3] IQM, XIV. 7.

"Blessed are you who are poor, for yours is the kingdom of God".

The materially poor, while paradigmatic of all kinds of deprivation, oppression and suffering, are also paradigmatic of those who are disposed to regard themselves as insignificant and unworthy and are radically humble.

It is only when material poverty is matched by this sense of insignificance and humility that there is blessedness. But this in no way means only the materially poor, nor are *all* the materially poor blessed. In God's inscrutable mercy the affluent who show humility and mourn their sins can also receive God's blessedness. Putting it this way is to seem to go against those who, starting from the inherent alienating effects of capitalism on labour, argue that poverty is structurally caused and, therefore, demands structural solutions such as socialism offers. However, in my view the Bible does not endorse any ready-made solution. Those who offer socialism as the solution are entering the realm of ideology with its value systems, and their sets of assumptions must be subject to the test of scriptural revelation.[4] In any case, my experience of socialism in Africa does not give me the confidence that socialism is the panacea for the structural difficulty. Besides, there is the oppressed and the oppressor in each and every one, rich and poor alike.

In any case, the poor, in so far as they are co-extensive with the godly who are set apart for God and his kingdom, have the kingdom of God. Of course, in the teaching of the New Testament the kingdom is only inaugurated in the ministry of Jesus and awaits its consummation. So it cannot be that the poor experience the kingdom in its fullness. But precisely because their behaviour and attitudes are consonant with the requirements of the kingdom, they are already beginning to enjoy it in anticipation. That "not yet" element is important, if the poor are not to rest on their oars. There is a point of accountability to the sovereign Lord for which all, rich and poor, must stand in

---

[4] I recognize that in taking this stance I will be criticized for reading the text from my own perspective. But who does not? Any reading of the Bible is conditioned by the human situation of the reader. Similarly the judgment as to what one is called to do is also conditioned by one's situation.

readiness. In other words, poverty, like the kingdom, cannot be allowed to be a status condition; it is a process. It is a straining towards the mark of Christ in community.

Before we leave off this first beatitude, I wish to bring us back to Psalm 34:6 and Proverbs 19:17. Psalm 34 thanks God for deliverance from tribulation. In that context the psalmist writes:

> The poor man called, and the Lord heard him;
> He saved him out of all his troubles.

The fortunate one who helps the less fortunate thereby establishes a sense of community. In that sense the social order should correspond to the moral order established by God.

Several of the beatitudes, especially those in the first stanza of the beatitudes, either flow out of or are expatiations on "Blessed are you who are poor". Let us turn to those relevant passages.

The second beatitude, "Blessed are they who mourn, for they shall be comforted" (Matt. 5:4), naturally follows from the first beatitude. How often do the poor not cry and mourn? Material poverty creates great anguish. But at a deeper level, the poor in the sense of the humble before God cry for God's mercy. Mourning and fasting are signs and symbols of true repentance, a turning to God, not its substitute. Here two passages should prove illuminating. The first, Isaiah 57:18-19a, reads:

> I have seen his ways but I will heal him
> I will guide him and restore comfort to him,
> creating praises on the lips of the mourners in Israel.

The context makes clear that the mourners are the contrite persons. It is the contrite, the humble before God, the poor, who have comfort. The other passage is Isaiah 61:1-2:

> The Spirit of the Sovereign Lord is on me,
> because the Lord has anointed me
> to preach good news to the poor.
> He has sent me to bind up the broken-hearted...
> to comfort all who mourn.

In the parallelism of the passage "the poor", "the broken-hearted", those "who mourn" are the same people. The prophet, seeing himself as fulfilling the mission of Israel, sees his mission as declaring God's promised salvation which, needless to say, has everything to do with the kingdom. The poor, the broken-hearted, the captives and the imprisoned are Israelites of the post-exilic community, not Israel as a whole. Thus the poor and mourners are the devout core of the faithful. It is they who have the promise of salvation and the kingdom. And so, "those who mourn" are the penitents who are disturbed by their own sinful state and that of the covenanted people of God who are called to live in community. These are the poor who know their inadequacies and mourn them.

In a very divided church, the poor see the scandal of the divisions as an insult to God and mourn them. Whoever understands that the church is the people of God has good reason to mourn the scandal of church disunity and to work for that unity in Christ. In an increasingly divided world marked by polarization between the haves and the have-nots, the rich and the poor, the North and the South, the poor will mourn the lack of a sense of community which God intends for the world God created. Mourning is not inactivity; precisely because they mourn, they take steps to correct the anomaly so that they can cease to mourn.

To such penitents there is in the saving purpose of God the assurance of forgiveness and, therefore, of comfort. In this regard Isaiah 57:17-18 is instructive: "Because of their sins of greed, I was indignant for a time and smote them and in anger hid my face... I will now heal them and guide them, repaying them with comfort — those of them who are sorry." Such people who experience comfort will have peace (cf. Isa. 57:19), while those who persist in their wickedness can never have peace (Isa. 57:20-21; cf. Isa. 61:1). Surely there are affluent people in the first as in the third world, who have financial resources to live a comfortable and secure life-style, who nevertheless feel oppressed and captive to contemporary values and structures. They feel lost and unable to cope with their circumstances and, in mourning their circumstances, turn to God. The poor include those who refuse to play God, to show penitence, a posture which results in forgiveness by God and this brings comfort, the comfort given by God.

The third beatitude: "Blessed are the *praeis*", the Greek word variously translated as the meek, the serene, the humble-minded, the humble, the gentle. It is not without interest that the Hebrew word behind *praeis* is *'anau* which is sometimes used as a synonym of *'ani*, one of the key words for poor in Hebrew. Commentators have drawn attention to the parallelism between this beatitude and Psalm 37:9-11, especially v.11:

> v. 9: For evil men will be cut off, but those who hope in the Lord will inherit the land.
> v.10: A little while, and the wicked will be no more; though you look for them, they will not be found.
> v.11: But the meek will inherit the land and enjoy great peace.

That Psalm seeks to encourage those who are depressed by the apparent success of the ungodly. The psalmist reminds them of God's retribution on the ungodly in due course. The meek who presently experience afflictions have hope which is assured and rooted in faith guaranteed and assured by God. The meek are those who, in spite of adversity, like the poor of the first beatitude, cling to their faith in the goodness and loving care of God for the righteous. They have unshakeable trust in the divine Providence through thick and thin. The poor who are serene shall inherit the earth. Human society is vitiated in its economic, cultural, social, political, religious dimensions by violence, manipulation, exploitation and ruthlessness. This situation is due to the lack of benevolence and mutual respect. The way out of this mess is gentleness, meekness, humble-mindedness, trust in God.

The promise made to the meek is the inheritance of the land. In its original context in Psalm 37 the land was the land of Israel, the promised land, the land of their forefathers which was to be restored to them, despite the present dire conditions. But here "land" is used metaphorically of the kingdom of God, the content of blessedness. This makes clearer still the link between the first beatitude and the third. Beyond the sense of spiritual need (cf. Matt. 5:3) there is the related attitude of unshakeable trust in God alone. The fullness of the kingdom of God is to be enjoyed by those who exercise absolute trust in God like the little children. As Mark 10:15-16 puts it: "Whoever fails to receive the kingdom of God like a little child, will not enter it at all. Taking them in his arms, he blessed them..."

The fourth beatitude has two versions: in Luke it runs: "Blessed are you who hunger now; you will be satisfied" (Luke 6:2a). In Matthew it reads: "Blessed are they who are hungry and thirsty for righteousness, for they shall be satisfied" (Matt. 5:6). In the way Luke states it, there is no special virtue in being physically hungry. Even the guerrilla who has to go hungry in his hideout or in the wilderness is fighting for justice which, whatever else it means, is decent living including being fed. But to hunger after righteousness is another matter. Matthew's version is an interpretation of Luke's reference to the hungry. The addition of "after righteousness" to hunger and thirst indicates that though these are perfectly natural and human cravings, in this context hunger and thirst are figurative as in such passages as Psalm 42:2, "My soul thirsts for God..."

The word "righteousness" is, of course, a crucial theological and religious term, especially in Matthew, which includes in its store of references "Seek first the kingdom of God and its righteousness" (Matt. 6:33) and "It becomes us to fulfill all righteousness" (Matt. 3:15). In its Old Testament usage it goes, if it is not synonymous, with expressions like God's demands, justification, salvation, victory. For example, in Isaiah 51:5,6,8 we read:

> My victory (righteousness) is near,
> my salvation is gone forth...
> My salvation shall abide for ever and
> my victory shall never be annulled...
> My victory shall be for ever and
> my salvation to all generations.

Righteousness is a moral quality. It also speaks of God's vindication of those who trust in him. The word "righteousness" in its Old Testament usage refers to "blessings conferred in Israel in token that its right is acknowledged and declared by God". [5] In its New Testament usage it is a gift of God issuing in forgiveness of sins and a promise of a share in eternal life, i.e. in blessedness. It refers to the demands of God on God's creation, especially the believers; it includes justice.

---

[5] J. Skinner, *The Book of the Prophet Isaiah*, Cambridge, Cambridge University Press, 1951, Vol. II, pp.240-242.

24

The word "righteousness" then has a rich range of meanings: moral quality, God's vindication of those who trust in God, gift of God as it becomes manifest in the forgiveness of sin. In this context, to hunger after righteousness is to commit oneself to doing the will of God. Such have their prayers answered by God and find inner satisfaction in having done God's will.

The four beatitudes represent one's pilgrimage in the kingdom of God. The poor are awakened to their inadequacy and moral bankruptcy; then they resolve to turn to God in repentance and are assured of divine forgiveness. They adopt an attitude of trust in God, earnestly longing for total righteousness or salvation. And they commit themselves to doing the will of God, particularly that humanity may live in community.

The ideas in the second stanza of the beatitudes are a further portraiture of the Christian in the image of God, the poor of whom the first beatitude speaks. Let us quickly run through them.

The fifth beatitude: "Blessed are the merciful, for they shall obtain mercy" (Matt. 5:7). Long before Jesus, the prophet Hosea had emphasized that Yahweh is the God of *chesed*. That word is important. There is no word in English which does justice to the rich variety of meanings of the Hebrew word. It is variously translated as mercy, love, loving-kindness, pity, etc. It is "kind-hearted actions that by spontaneous love and the faithful meeting of responsibilities create or establish a sense of community". [6]

First, it is referred to in the context of the covenant relationship between Yahweh and Yahweh's people. It is the quality of the God who elects Israel and is the Lord of saving history. Second, love is the characteristic of the relationship between Yahweh and his people. It is expressed as unalterable commitment and intimate relationship. The signs of this relationship include grace, pity, reconciliation, etc. It is intimate solidarity between a person and God. Third, precisely because love is seen in the context of a covenanted relationship, it becomes also the demand of God on God's people. God's quality of *chesed* becomes the quality demanded of the covenanted people of

---

[6] H.W. Wolff, *A Commentary on the Book of the Prophet Hosea*, Philadelphia, Fortress Press, 1974, p.52.

God. It is a relationship between members of the covenant community, which demands care for the other person, and justice. It is the principle of social ethics and the foundation for the nation's economic and political peace. Thus the mercy envisaged here is about relationships, about community, about acts and actions, not just some emotional expression.

If mercy is the principle of social ethics, it is also the foundation of word and worship, law and cult: "I desire loving-kindness and not sacrifices, and the knowledge of God more than burnt offerings" (Hos. 6:6). The context in which this was said is worthy of note. The days in which Hosea prophesied were a time of political security and economic plenty (Hosea 2:4-17; 3:1-5). But with it had grown corruption, injustice, wickedness and ruthlessness. Alongside that was a flourishing cult (Hos. 4:1-5:7). The cult, like any ecumenical and mission-ary task, should seek to bring about reconciliation on the basis of God's redemption and should be an expectation of the new life which God promises. Thus good life and cult should not be alternatives. Such a message is most apposite for an imperfect world marked by ruthlessness and cut-throat competition, a world in which the poor like the righteous are surrounded by vice.

Karl Barth has a book with the title *Zwischen der Zeiten*, literally "Between the Times". It is about living between times, this time and eternity. I use that phrase to suggest that the call to show mercy is a call to live the eternal life of the kingdom of God in this temporal and temporary scene. That was what those who were put on the right of the king in the parable of the sheep and the goats did. They lived eternity in their dealings with the naked, the imprisoned, the hungry. They were the merciful ones because they knew that the covenant relationship with God and the community demanded caring acts of mercy. Mercy, then, is a quality of the poor in spirit. As long as there is poverty, human beings are invited to show the quality of mercy towards the less fortunate. In so doing they do not only rise up to their true humanity but also show their appreciation of the loving kindness of God showered on them.

The merciful have the promise that they will obtain mercy. This is a theme that comes up several times in Judaism. For example, according to the Babylonian Talmud *Shabbath* 151b, "whoever has mercy on people will obtain pity from heaven". So to speak, the reward for showing pity is that one also becomes a recipient of God's pity. But showing pity to others is also a condition for receiving the pity of others and of God. What sounds like a reward is also a condition. Two biblical passages in the gospel elaborate this theme.

In the Lord's Prayer we read: "Forgive us our debts as we have forgiven our debtors" (Matt. 6:12). Having forgiven others, one may have the courage to ask for God's forgiveness. In Ecclesiasticus 28:2 we read: "Forgive your neighbour his wrong-doing then, when you pray, your sins will be forgiven." In other words, the best proof that one seriously desires reconciliation with God is that the sinner himself/herself forgives fellow human beings. Forgiveness of sin is a quality of mercy, but it is also shown in gratitude for one's experiences of or expectations of the forgiveness of God.

The other passage is Matthew 18:23-35, the parable of the unforgiving servant who, though forgiven much, could not forgive a small debt owed to him. Those who have not learnt to forgive or show mercy are incapable of experiencing forgiveness and mercy. In a world in which the weak are pushed to the wall, in a world in which politicians use their power to put down opponents ruthlessly, in a world in which some people are understandably blinded by and captive to hatred, bitterness, etc. such a message needs to be constantly recalled as also standing in the tradition of our Christian teaching. Retaliation and revenge have no place in the life of those who are committed to the kingly rule of God.

In many an African country, cliques holding the reigns of power have done much violence to their own people, sometimes for the simple reason that the latter have succeeded in life. Sooner or later, and as sure as day follows night, they fall from power. And then it becomes an issue what to do with such people who have manifestly misbehaved so badly. In that situation Christians still need to ask: what does it mean for Jesus to say "turn the other cheek"? What is the nature and shape of forgiveness in a context where the rulers, the powerful and the rich have definitely misbehaved? Forgiveness does not mean acquiescing in evil; neither is it being an accessory to wickedness. On the other hand, hate and unrelenting vengeance are self-destructive. It is between these two alternatives that mercy comes into its own. It is the characteristic of the one who would act to demolish the kingdom of Satan but not in a spirit of revenge. No nation can survive and live in peace when there is no mercy.

One does not wait till the liberation before one begins to talk of mercy. It is a crucial task to prepare our nations for that day of liberation with this message of mercy which does not make us opt out of our obligation to resist evil but does not either make us bitterly vengeful. The desire for justice is not in dispute. But never shall it be allowed to become a selfish concern. Ill-will should not determine one's response to ill treatment. In resisting evil, there is at the same time a need to desire for even one's enemies the supreme and ultimate good.

The sixth beatitude relates to "the pure in heart". They "shall see God" (Matt. 5:8). This, as scholars have pointed out, echoes Psalm 24:4:

> Who may ascend the hill of the Lord?
> Who may stand in his holy place?
> He who has clean hands and a *pure heart*,
> Who does not lift up his soul to an idol
> or swear by what is false.
> He will receive blessing from the Lord
> and vindication from God his Saviour.

That passage is about the basic moral requirement: freedom from vain and evil thoughts, purity of mind and action. Lifting the soul to an idol is worshipping or adoring emptiness, vanity, fraud or deceit. The "heart" in its biblical usage is not the emotional seat of the person; rather it is the intellectual centre of a human being. Thus the psalmist insists that a basic condition of communion with God is the single-mindedness of the conse-crated life. Important as cultic practices may be as aids to recognizing the sovereignty of God, the crucial thing is that cultic practice and inward and external integrity shall under-score to the religious person that his/her life is dedicated to God. Single-minded devotion to God's rule and its righteousness is at once a basic condition of communion with God and a spiritual bond. "The pure in heart" then are a good example of the poor, those who are truthful and single-mindedly devoted to God.

They are characterized by absolute sincerity and mutual trust. No one can build a just world without this quality.

Our journalists, politicians, teachers and power-seekers need to hear this message! The diplomatic use of truth and dealing in half-truths cannot lead to the kingly rule of God. The truly poor in spirit must practise true religion which is described as being "pure in heart".

The seventh beatitude is: "Blessed are the peace-makers, for they shall be called God's sons" (Matt. 5:9). Living as we are under the threat of nuclear holocaust, and suffering the ravages of civil wars in Africa as in Latin America, and the effects of polarization and divisive trends in politics, peace is indeed a most welcome theme for the normal human being. Again and again, it is asserted in the Bible that the mission of the people of God is to promote peace (Isa. 52:7; 57:18-21; Eph. 2:13f.). That peace is as individual as it is societal, as internal as it is external. Peace is the state of security and wellbeing both outward and inward. Peace is several things together — wholeness, harmony, wellbeing, a truly happy life, a blessing which includes everything that constitutes the richness of a happy life. These are the indices of peace and it is only right conduct that can lead to peace. The wicked destroy their own opportunities for peace. But peace is the work of healing performed by God (cf. Isa. 52; 57). The gospel should aid and aim at peace of heart which is the acceptance of ourselves. And as St Augustine said: "Our hearts are restless until they find their rest in thee." The confessional or penance, abuses apart, is designed to be an aid to this acceptance of ourselves. In working for peace in the world, we share the quality of Jesus Christ, the Prince of Peace, and truly become children of God.

The seventh beatitude enjoins on all Christians and men and women of good will the commitment to promoting reconciliation between families, nations, races, tribes, sexes, religions. How it puts Christians to shame! How many times have religious people not gone to war in the name of religion? How disgraceful that the people of God who claim to be charged with a ministry of reconciliation (2 Cor. 5:19f.) are themselves so hopelessly divided! The ecumenical movement is neither a luxury nor an exercise in expediency; it is a matter of the credibility of the church as the harbinger of peace. May God forgive our foolish ways and hasten the day of a reconciled people of God and of reconciled races and tribes and sexes.

But let us be careful not to promote cheap peace and reconciliation. True peace comes from humble and honest engagement with the integrity of the other person in harmonious dialogue. Nothing is swept under the carpet. And for us Christians reconciliation is an indispensable condition of true worship (Matt. 5:23f.), and it is a priority. It is personal in approach but at the same time concerned with conditions and systems. That is why the cosmopolitan and political arena is and should be the concern of religious persons. For the same reason the ideologies of apartheid and tribalism are sins which deny the ministry of reconciliation of the church and must be resisted firmly.

And it is precisely because of this beatitude that the document published by the World Council of Churches, *Baptism, Eucharist and Ministry*, is worthy of study. That document represents the efforts of a repentant divided church to reach the reconciliation of brothers and sisters in Christ as a step towards summing up all things in Christ. I do not believe BEM is perfect because, for example, the ministry of women is not exactly faced squarely. But for all its shortcomings it is worthy of committed study as at least a good starting-point for beginning to sum up all things in Christ.

And so finally we come to the eighth beatitude, which speaks of those persecuted for the sake of righteousness and Christ. The poor who are dedicated to God and God's rule are in constant danger of Satan who prowls around like a roaring lion seeking whom he/she may devour (1 Pet. 5:8). We cannot live the life of eternity in this temporal scene without pain. One of the most painful things about ministry is how wrong interpretations and motives can be put on one's actions. Christ himself was called a deceiver who would lead others astray. It is not uncommon for Christians to be dubbed as rebels and subversives. True witness of Christ almost invariably carries with it persecution of one kind or another.

In the ancient Roman empire as in a number of countries today, Christians have suffered on account of the hope of their calling. In Nazi Germany Martin Niemöller and Dietrich Bonhoeffer suffered for the sake of the gospel but, as we believe, not in vain. In Zaire Christians have suffered because

of the political ideology of *authenticité*. In Iran Christians are
persecuted in the name of Islam. The poor who are committed to
Christ suffer. Indeed, suffering is a *sine qua non* of being in
Christ. But no *force majeure* can absolve the Christian from his/
her witness. And by standing fast in the faith despite persecution
one "sanctifies the Holy Name", declaring in no uncertain terms
that one is for Christ and God. To witness to Christ through
martyrdrom and persecution is evidence of one's devotion to
and zeal for the Lord. Such must count themselves privileged —
blessed because they are called upon to witness for Christ.

This survey of the beatitudes has attempted to argue that
seven of the eight beatitudes are, so to speak, portraitures of
what is involved in being poor in spirit. In describing the
disciples of Jesus as "poor in spirit", there is no dualism of
present poverty and future glory. Indeed, ongoing effort in
Christian living in the here and now is what guarantees any
future. In being poor the believer follows Christ who, "although
he was rich, yet he became poor for your sakes, so that by his
poverty you might become rich" (2 Cor. 8:9). Further, any
passive or romantic ideas of poverty are excluded; rather, the
poverty is about commitment to a radical discipleship and
abandonment to God.

> All too often the poor are equated with the less fortunate, i.e. the
> developing world, the victims of exploitation, victims of racism,
> sexism, and religious intolerance. There is no doubt that the word
> includes those who are held in contempt, such as publicans and sinners
> (Mark 2:16), and prostitutes (Matt. 21:32). But it is not exhausted by
> the victims of oppression. It covers those who have notoriously failed
> to observe the commandments of God, as well as those despised today.
> The circle of the "poor" is even wider. That becomes clear when we
> collect the designations and imagery with which Jesus characterizes
> them. He calls them the hungry, those who weep, the sick, those who
> labour, those who bear burdens, the least, the simple, the lost, the
> sinners. The word covers those under outward oppression as in Luke as
> well as those with inner need as in Matthew. [7]

Needless to say, I am arguing for the need to get away from
the idealization of poverty and indiscriminate damnation of the

---

[7] See J.S. Pobee, "Church and Community", *African and Asian Contributions to
Contemporary Theology*, ed. J.S. Mbiti, Geneva, WCC, 1977, p.87.

rich. If indeed "the earth is the Lord's and all that is in it" and if indeed God's love goes out to all and God punishes sin wherever it is found, then it cannot be said that *God* has a bias against the rich. We can only say, after Jesus, that it is often harder for the rich to enter the kingdom of God.

And it is not as if all poor persons are righteous. The poor also cheat; they oppress their wives; they tell lies just like the rich. Here indeed is a warning against reading "Blessed are the poor" out of context.

At this point we must turn to the modern use of the term "the poor". One of the important legacies of Latin American liberation theology is its insights with regard to the poor. The historic Puebla declaration by the Latin American bishops (1979) discerned that the gospel of Christ contains a striking preferential option for the poor:

> The exact meaning of this option is to recognize the privileged status of the poor as the new and emerging historical subject which will carry on the Christian project in the world. The poor, here, are not understood simply as those in need, they are in need but they are also the group with a historical strength, a capacity for change and a potential for evangelization... The church is directed to all, but begins with the poor, from their desires and struggles. Thus arise the essential themes of the church: social change creating a more just society; human rights interpreted as the rights of the poor majority; social justice and integral liberation, achieved primarily through socio-historical freedom and concrete services on behalf of the disinherited of this world and so on.

Thus wrote Leonardo Boff in his book *Church, Charisma and Power*. [8] One can only say Amen to all this, even if one may not exactly use the language that liberation theologians tend to use. But in spite of divergence of language which is all part of being a world of peoples from different races, sexes, cultures etc., we are agreed that "Blessed are you who are poor; for yours is the kingdom of God", and "Blessed are the poor in spirit, for theirs is the kingdom of heaven" have a challenging message for us today.

---

[8] London, SCM Press, 1985, pp.9-10.

3. Woe to You, Rich

We have emphasized that the existence of areas of poverty in the human community is a sign that God's purpose and designs with regard to the community of men and women and of races, classes and creeds are not realized. Besides, it is a fact that the policies and activities of the rich, whether persons or nations, make others poor. It is therefore meaningless to think of the poor in isolation and apart from the rich. And in any case I believe it to be God's will to save all humankind, the rich included. Therefore I wish now to turn to the rich.

In the Gospel of Luke (6:24-26), the beatitudes are immediately followed by the four "woes":

> Alas for you who are rich; you have had your time of happiness. Alas for you who are well-fed now; you shall go hungry. Alas for you who laugh now; you shall mourn and weep. Alas for you when all speak well of you; just so did their fathers treat the false prophets.

The four woes are about owners of property and those who make riches their source of happiness and satisfaction. In that context wealth implies false values and, consequently, the so-called rich become spiritually destitute. The rich have earthly success and have reached their own self-set goals and, in so doing, declare their independence from God. In the process they are really separated from God. The rich find joy and pleasure in pastimes which the world offers. They prefer popularity with people to God's favour; they strive to gain the goodwill of all; they compromise and ignore what is right. But worship of self and the cultivation of the friendship of this world are not compatible with discipleship (cf. 1 Kings 22:5-28).

The qualities we are warned against seem to be different manifestations of the opposite of being poor. The poor are not well-fed, and it represents an economic view of wealth and poverty. The poor do not normally laugh. In terms of material resources they are in distress and anxiety, wondering whence the next meal is coming.

The rich are expected to be well-fed and laughing; they are happy. And yet sometimes they are in reality and morally bankrupt and unhappy and miserable. In South Africa the whites under the apartheid system are socially and materially much better off than the blacks. But as we said earlier, either they suffer from the "black danger" or they have become insensitive to human suffering and in the process have ceased to be human. Thus they are dehumanized and pauperized.

In theory the materially rich have everything and can afford to be merry. And yet, ironically they not infrequently have no contentment. David had everything and yet he contrived the death of Uriah the Hittite so as to take Bathsheba (2 Sam. 11-12). In our own day it is not uncommon to see rich men and women who try to buy friendship or in their greed become prisoners of their wealth with the result that they have no real happiness. In Africa, men of power and influence like politicians and rich men apparently do no wrong until they lose their positions of power, and then every crime is laid at their doorstep. Nkrumah of Ghana was apparently the fountain of goodness until he was overthrown in February 1966. At that stage he was accused of being not only a dictator but also a rogue and a thief.

Of course, as Luke states the "woes", the setbacks are an eschatological phenomenon in the sense that it is in the kingdom of God that the so-called rich will be judged harshly. A number of questions come to one's mind. Is this not the other side of what the Marxist will call the celestial dope offered by Christians? On this we have already commented. The point here is that salvation, eternal life, kingdom of God and whatever other expressions we may use to describe our hope is never to be identified with wellbeing or the sum total of satisfied human needs. In any case, the biblical hope is not just other-worldly, because the ultimates are related to the present time, affecting the actual realities of life here and now. However, for the present the more important question is: how come the rich are threatened with such a bleak future? In search of an answer, let us proceed to a study of the story of the rich young ruler (Mark 10:17-31; Matt. 19:16-30; Luke 18:18-30).

The rich young ruler

That story is all too familiar to be recounted in detail here. But let us put our exegesis in context. A rich man went to Jesus in search of "eternal life" (Mark 10:17, Matt. 19:16; Luke 18:18), which is otherwise known as the kingdom of God or salvation. This man was blessed with riches but he was also eager for salvation as is evidenced by the fact that he ran up to Jesus (Mark 10:17). He knelt before Jesus (Mark 10:17). That posture, seen in the light of contemporary practice, shows that he considered Jesus as a venerable rabbi. And Jesus would not dispute the rich man's piety. Perhaps Jesus was not travelling with those who would say all property is acquired by theft! As the texts puts it, Jesus liked this rich man who had been struggling to live by the will of God as expressed in the Ten Commandments (Mark 10:21). But precisely here we see the weakness of the rich man. Three things were wrong with him.

First, the rich man was confusing the demands of the Jewish church-state with the demands of conscience and righteousness (Mark 10:19; Matt. 19:18; Luke 18:20; cf. Ex. 20:12-26; Deut. 5:16,20; 24:14; Lev. 19:18). It is true that the ten commandments had a central place in Judaism because they were believed to be an expression of the divine will. Obedience of the commandments is a test of human goodness. But the rich man adopted a mechanical and perhaps one-dimensional view of salvation. Lochman has some perceptive words on this mechanical attitude to salvation. "Salvation is found neither in a system nor as a system but only wherever real life, freedom and happiness shatter the salvation systems and the planned and the predictable can expect to be disturbed. Resurrection? Judgment? Grace?... These incisive questions, particularly the reference to resurrection, judgment and grace... bring us to the second aspect of the alienation of salvation in the life of society and the church, namely the one-dimensional view of salvation. All salvation systems and machines have this tendency. A one-dimensional view of salvation enables them to operate more smoothly, 'interference free' with 'painful' (or agreeable) 'precision'. Undimensional man is far easier to direct and control. Herbert Marcuse's analysis of human alienation along these lines is therefore to be taken very seriously. It fits all salvation machines, both Eastern style and Western." [1]

The attitude of the rich man in the story of Jesus is representative of the many good and "decent" Christians who *de facto* exclude the "interference factor" by limiting the scope

---

[1] See J. Lochman, *Reconciliation and Liberation*, Belfast, Christian Journals Ltd, 1980, p.16.

of such factors as faith, God, judgment and resurrection. In simple terms, salvation has two dimensions: a horizontal one which struggles for the solution of historical social problems and a vertical one which seeks it in individualistic and metaphysical terms. The rich man is a type of verticalist, and this one-dimensional view of salvation is a distortion of the good news of salvation. The economic, political and cultural life of society is not just the business of secular communities, it is also the business of religious persons. The one who would have eternal life can never be rightly insulated from secular questions; for such a person no area of human life can be immune to the message of salvation and the demands of God. The rich man in our story had so concentrated on the mechanical aids to salvation as to lose sight of their original goal.

Second, in his devotion to the ten commandments or the demands of the "church", he had missed their true goal of being called to be human. This comes out clearly when it is said that the rich man became very sorry when he was asked to give away his wealth to the poor (Mark 10:21). Religious practices without a human face and a feeling heart are a denial of true religion. How the message of the eighth century prophets comes into its own! They castigated precisely those religious persons who showed no sensitivity to injustice and no passion for justice. By that insensitivity they were already in sin and stood under the judgment of God. G.P. Maclear, commenting on the young ruler's question "what shall I do?" writes as follows: "The question betrays his fundamental error. Not by doing, but by being, was an entrance into it to be obtained." [2] Furthermore, one is struck by one item of the ten commandments given in free form: "Defraud not" (v.19). It means: "Do not deprive anyone of what is theirs." In other words, the point of the individual items of law is to be your brother's or sister's brother or sister, caring for and securing his/her best interests. For a rich person such an injunction has tremendous pointed force. Has the rich man's wealth been used to secure the best interests of the less fortunate?

---

[2] *The Gospel According to St Mark*, Cambridge, Cambridge University Press, 1883, p.112.

Third, the rich man had become a slave of his wealth. That is the message of the comment that "his face fell and he went away with a heavy heart" (Mark 10:22). Wealth can be a heavy liability in the movement towards the kingdom of God. "How hard it will be for the wealthy to enter the kingdom of God!" (Mark 10:23). "It is easier for a camel to pass through the eye of a needle than for a rich man to enter the kingdom of God" (Mark 10:25). In this figurative language Jesus with characteristic insight draws attention to the dangers attendant on wealth. It is not that wealth is inherently evil; rather the danger is that it can come between a human being and God because one begins to love it so much that he/she no longer enjoys it. As the author of 1 Timothy puts it, "those who want to be rich fall into temptations and snares and many foolish harmful desires which plunge human beings into ruin and perdition. The love of money is the root of all evil things, and there are some who in reaching for it have wandered from the faith and spiked themselves on many thorny griefs" (6:9-10).

It is not money by itself but love of money which is the problem and the danger. The love of money is described by Ecclesiastes as vanity or emptiness (5:10ff.). The point, simply put, is this: the demands of the kingdom take precedence over wealth and its demands. And for precisely that reason Jesus commends those who have given up everything — family and property — in the interests of the kingdom (Mark 10:28-31).

The rich fool

The warning against the dangers in wealth is a sustained theme in Luke's Gospel. Let us take two examples from Luke 12:13-21 and Luke 16:19-31. The first one, the parable of the rich fool, is told to warn against greed: "Beware! Be on your guard against greed of every kind" (Luke 12:15). The rich fool had become a prisoner of his wealth. He lived money, he slept money, he dreamed money. He longed for more money. Everything was money. His primary concern was the acquisition of more and more wealth. His god was his wealth. He was scheming all the time to increase his possessions: "I will pull down my storehouses and build them bigger" (Luke 12:18). He was thinking all the time of the growth of his business and his increase. Those in business want profits. Profit-making is essential for the financial administration of the economy. That is why Jesus commended those who made profit with their talents. So what needs to be carefully addressed is the legitimate limits of legitimate profit. Certainly cut-throat profit-making is unacceptable. Loose, radical talk is no help to clarity on this matter. But religious people will seek to balance profit-making with genuine concern for the genuine wellbeing of others.

Two comments are of particular interest for us. First, Jesus points out the ludicrous nature of our preoccupation with wealth. Struggling assiduously to amass wealth, one merely helps someone else to enjoy it (Luke 12:20). The message is that at the end of the day there will be some distance between you and your wealth, for possessions are ephemeral and temporal. The further implication is that it is therefore folly to rely on wealth and possessions. Greed and covetousness only serve to keep one away from the kingdom of God or at the very least serve to make difficult one's progress towards the kingdom of God. A person's life can never be his/her own.

The second comment is contained in the concluding words of that parable: "That is how it is with the man who amasses wealth for himself and remains a pauper in the sight of God" (Luke 12:21). To understand this fully, one must go back to some of the Jewish beliefs. One of particular interest is related to the story of Job. That story begins in the heavenly court with a dialogue between God and Satan, who was then a kind of attorney-general at the court of God. God comments on the sound and exemplary religiosity of Job (Job 1:8). To that comment Satan replies: "Has not Job good reason to be God-fearing? Have you not hedged him round on every side with your protection, him and his family and all his possessions? Whatever he does you have blessed, and his herds have increased beyond measure" (Job 1:9-10). In other words, according to this tradition wealth and prosperity are indicative of good standing with God. The rest of the Book of Job is a kind of protest against this theology: it argues that it is possible for a righteous person to suffer abject poverty. Jesus also states that wealth is not necessarily an index of good standing with God. A wealthy person can sometimes be a pauper in God's sight because of the person's wrong priorities and practices. Thorough-going materialism is alienation from God and leads to emptiness of life. Thus this parable reinforces the point made earlier of the need for a holistic view of life, the need for the material to be balanced with the spiritual, the horizontal by the vertical.

The story of the rich young ruler illustrates the problem of covetousness to which the rich are prone. Covetousness is acquiring wealth for its own sake. Wealth is not the rich man's sin but it had become an occasion for covetousness which is idolatry, the cardinal sin (cf. Col. 3:5; Luke 16:9). It is the Gadarene rush of materialism, a danger to human wholeness because of its total insensitivity to spiritual matters. The story of the rich fool can be rewritten under the title: "Where your investment is, there is your heart." In seeking more riches, he not only becomes greedy but also sets up false gods of contentment and pleasure and power. He forgets God the giver and forgets also the poor for whose sake he is entrusted with the stewardship of riches. The rich then stand in danger of greed, idolatry and inhumanity. And so, woe to the rich.

Lazarus and Dives

The parable of the Rich Man and Lazarus (Luke 16:19-31) is also instructive in its own way. It reads like a skit on the experiences of our own day. The rich man lived in comfort and appears to have steadily grown more comfortable, rather like the nations of the North that get richer and richer, while the poorer nations of the South get poorer and poorer every day. The parable tells the familiar story of the stark inequalities of life, of the growing gulf between the rich and the poor.

The poor man, Lazarus, was covered with sores. That detail is interesting: sores may be caused by many factors, such as lack of sanitation or lack of nutrition. But we may dare to suggest that the story of Lazarus is a story about society's responsibility vis-à-vis poverty. Society produces the poor and makes many poor. Worse still is society's insensitivity to the plight of the poor. This sore-ridden Lazarus was laid at the gate of the rich; but he was ignored by the rich man and by those who went in and out. In other words, the rich man and his friends were selfish and hard-hearted persons who ignored the wretched of the earth. As if that were not enough, the dogs used to come and lick his sores (v.21). Lazarus had no protection even against the dogs. Lazarus is the paradigm of the poor and the weak.

The story of Lazarus is indeed like the story of the rich and the poor nations today. At one level there is today a greater sensitivity to the plight of the less fortunate. The transfer of resources from the North to the South through the United Nations Organization and other bodies is a good illustration of it. But, as it is also well known, as a result of an unjust international economic order and oppressive structures this supposed concern for the poor is ineffective, and even counter-productive. It only succeeds in pauperizing the countries of the South further. So the question to put to the countries of the North as much as to the rich within the countries of the South is: "You seem to care; you give to the poor. But is your charity good enough? Is your seeming concern really meeting the truest needs of the less fortunate? Are the structures of relationships, economic and otherwise, in the best interests of the poor?" The message is clear: wealth is held on trust from God to be used to help the less fortunate in life. With wealth goes responsibility for the less fortunate. When the rich abdicate that deep sense of responsibility for the poor they come under the judgment of God. Selfish absorption in one's own pleasure and indifference to the misery around — that is the undoing of the rich.

Another message that comes through from this parable is that one's standing in the kingdom of God is determined to some extent by how one lives in the here and now. Dives went to hell. One factor in determining his consignment to hell is "in your life-time you received your good things" (Luke 16:25). That may suggest that it is his wealth *per se* that was his undoing. A life of luxury carries with it its own dangers. But perhaps the more interesting point is Dives's insensitivity to the poor man at his gate (Luke 16:20-21). It could be suggested further that it was not only mere insensitivity; he saw to it that the poor man was denied the crumbs that fell from his table. In relating to the poor Lazarus, Dives's judgment was being written. By not treating his wealth as something held on trust from God to be used for God's glory and for the wellbeing of the less fortunate, he consigned himself to hell. Here is an illustration of what the parable of the sheep and the goats says: Christ confronts human beings in everyday events and ordinary persons, the thirsty, the hungry, the naked, the stranger, the ill, and those in prison (Matt. 25:31-46). The rich man learnt his lesson too late.

On the other hand, Lazarus went to Abraham's side, i.e. paradise. The reason for Lazarus's admission to paradise was God's mercy on one who had it rough during his life-time (Luke 16:25). No reference is made to Lazarus's goodness or upright living. As the story stands now, a place in paradise is a kind of compensation for suffering on earth. In that sense the story is the illustration of the beatitude that the poor inherit the kingdom of God. Blessed are you who hunger now; you will be satisfied. Blessed are you who weep now; for you will laugh (Luke 6:21).

The after-life dialogue between the rich man and Abraham is also revealing. First, the rich man wants Lazarus sent over to give him water. Then he wants him sent to his relations. He still seems to think Lazarus is a person of no account; he alone matters, and his relatives; and Lazarus must serve his purposes. Wealth breeds contempt and arrogance.

Let us draw the threads together. Woe is pronounced on the rich not so much because they have wealth but because of the real dangers attendant on riches. If one sees one's wealth as an end in itself, one becomes a slave to wealth and develops false priorities which can only serve to exclude him/her from the kingdom of God. The security that wealth gives is only a mirage; for the only sure refuge is God.

Furthermore, wealth is a trust which involves responsibility for the less fortunate. It is to the one who ignores one's responsibilities to the less fortunate that Jesus rightly says: "Woe to you, rich." Spirituality is not so much a metaphysical quality as a quality of response to the call and challenges of God in everyday life. The woes of Luke 6:24-26 are not so much a curse as expressions of pity for those who display those qualities which exclude them from the kingdom of God, qualities like self-satisfaction and pride which *tend* to be the besetting sins of the wealthy, though not exclusive to them.

Such an interpretation may well appear reactionary in our times, for it is normal these days to castigate and rule out of court the rich *per se*. Many refuse to see any good in the rich and would talk as if all property is theft. It is true that in a wrong-headed and iniquitous world system the poor get poorer and the rich richer at the expense of the poor. The moves of the

Organization of Petroleum Exporting Countries vis-à-vis oil prices and politics meant, for example, that at least 40 percent of the foreign exchange of several African countries like Ghana, Senegal and Tanzania, was spent on oil. The direct consequence for these countries was tragic. Either it put a strain on balance of payments, or they had to borrow heavily as a kind of holding operation. In either approach the people, like the nations, became poorer. The selfishness of states made things worse: when the rich nations had to adjust to the OPEC prices, they did so in a manner that brought a collapse of primary commodity prices, which adversely affected the poor countries. [3] The international financial markets controlled by the North determine the patterns of distribution of even recycled oil surpluses. In the face of these and several other factors which suggest that the poor nations are still exploited, it may sound very odd to argue that wealth is not the problem but how it is used.

Perhaps at this point we must address the question of whether or not there is any hope. But for the present let me say that my reading of the Bible does not make it possible for me to condemn riches as such. According to the Akan of Ghana, *nsa nyina nse*, i.e. all the fingers are not the same. Some are short, others long, etc. They also say *moko nyina mpata mbir*, i.e. peppers do not all ripen at the same time. This insight that we cannot all be the same seems to me to be consonant with the biblical insights from Job on whom God had showered wealth. It is consonant with the biblical message of the responsibility of the rich to the poor, for which the mechanism of charity was an established institution in Jewish society. So if it is the biblical message that we seek to preach, I am convinced that while ill-gotten gain should be denounced, and while the insensitivity of the rich to the poor needs to be condemned, these are not the same as condemning wealth as such. So then the task is to warn the rich against ill-gotten gain and against their lack of sensitivity to the plight of the poor, and to invite them to realize themselves as genuine human beings who must live in a community of love, and with respect for the integrity of the other person. For that reason I wish to underline that saying that some

---

[3] See Charles Elliott, *Pains of Ungrowth*, London, Catholic Missionary Education Centre, 1983, p.83.

will be rich and others poor is no excuse for fatalism and condescending charity.

Again, it means that religious people must spare no effort to detect wicked structures that pauperize peoples and help forge structures that foster justice and righteousness and truth. That is also a ministry which the people of God owe to the world, the rich and the poor. Such a ministry has the goal of building community in which rich and poor complement each other meaningfully and in genuine self-fulfilment.

My ruminations on "Woe to you, rich" have been inadequate. I have no apology to make for it. For as it is more and more acknowledged, theological reflection should not start from abstractions but from people's experiences. And I have never been rich and cannot enter into the message vis-à-vis the rich completely. But one is emboldened to point out that those things said in this chapter are similar to sentiments in St Ambrose, the celebrated bishop of Milan in the fourth century A.D. in his *de Nabuthe*. [4] He wrote as follows:

> How far, you rich people, will you carry your insane cupidity?... Why do you reject nature's partnership of goods, and claim possession of nature for yourselves? The earth was established to be in common for all, why do you rich alone arrogate it to yourselves as your rightful property?... Rich man, do you not know how poor you really are; the more you have, the more you want, and whatever you may acquire, you nevertheless remain as needy as before. Avarice is inflamed by gain, not diminished by it...
>
> How many men are killed to produce the means of your enjoyment? A deadly thing is your greed, and deadly your luxury. One man falls to death from a roof in order that you may have your big granaries. Another tumbles from the top of a high tree while seeking for certain kinds of grapes, so that you may have the right wine for your banquet. Another is drowned in the sea while making sure that fish or oysters shall not be lacking on your table. Another is beaten to death before your eyes, if he happens to have displeased you... The avaricious man is always the loser of abundant harvests, since low prices of foodstuffs beat down his gains. To mankind in general it is fertility that is advantageous; only to the avaricious man is sterility profitable. He is better pleased with high prices than with abundant commodities; and he prefers to have something of

---

[4] Cf. Migne Patrologia Latina XIV.

which he is the sole vendor, rather than something which he must sell in competition with all the other vendors. Look at him! — fearful lest a surplus of grain should accumulate and the excess which the store-houses cannot hold should be handed over to the needy, and the poor thus get a chance of some benefit. The rich man claims the products of the earth for his own not because he wants to use them himself but in order that he may deny them to others...

These words were written in the fourth century. Yet they are most appropriate for today.

4. Hope for the Rich?
Today, "Salvation has Come to this House"

There has been a trend in theological circles in recent years to idealize poverty and to condemn the rich outright. While appreciating the contextual factors in such condemnation, we should not forget that in the biblical tradition there is no such idealization of poverty. The woes uttered against the rich are not curses on them but warnings against the dangers attendant on riches, and expressions of pity for those who have the heavy baggage of wealth. So I wish to examine two parables peculiar to Luke which seem to throw some light on the fate of the rich. I refer to the story of Zacchaeus (Luke 19:1-10) and the parable of the Pharisee and the Publican (Luke 18:9-14).

The Pharisee and the Publican

The parable of the Pharisee and the Publican was originally "aimed at those who were sure of their own goodness and looked down on everyone else" (Luke 18:9). A Pharisee and a tax-collector went to the temple to pray. The Pharisee was a busy adherent of Yahweh, one whose external behaviour was meticulously religious. Whereas according to Deuteronomy 14:23 and Leviticus 27:30-32 tithes were to be paid on corn, wine, oil and animals, this pious Pharisee went the extra mile to pay tithes on all his income. Again, like the strictest and most pious Jews he fasted twice a week, on Mondays and Thursdays. This constituted what in the Latin religious language is called *opus supererogationis*, a work that went beyond what was required and was a mark of holiness and special devotion to God. There is no doubt then about the man's supereminent piety.

However, his piety contained the seeds of sin. He was proud of it and consequently passed a vote of confidence on himself rather than waiting for God's judgment. His prayer of thanksgiving turns out to be an expression of self-congratulation and conspicuous piety. One passes quickly from admiration of oneself to denigration of others. The Pharisee's religiosity led him to show contempt for the tax-collector (Luke 18:11). Thus he was guilty of the cardinal sin of arrogance by implication. Humility is an essential quality for entering the kingdom of God. To be poor in spirit, whatever else it is, involves humility and eschewing every temptation to arrogance.

Seen in that light the trouble with the Pharisee was his pride, daring to establish a claim on God on the basis of his indisputable piety. He was self-righteous, haughty, self-satisfied and contemptuous of others. One lesson we may draw is that piety, as expressed in meticulous pursuit of the demands of religious institutions, is not the same as being "poor in spirit".

The attitude of the tax-collector is revealing. Because of the violence and extortion that accompanied their duty, not to mention the fact that they were in the service of the hated imperial rulers, tax collectors were considered despicable sinners. It could be assumed that he was not without some substance, ill-gotten gain most probably. But he was a deeply repentant sinner who took refuge in God's mercy rather than God's justice. In his prayer he was lifting his sub-conscious to God; there was no suggesion of the boldness and pride that characterized the Pharisee. Crying for mercy in a context of prayer, one seeks in humility for the covering of one's sins so as to be reconciled truly to God and to fellow human beings.

However, the more interesting point is that neither his occupation nor his ill-gotten gains by themselves put him beyond the pale. Once he showed a sense of contrition and penitence and humility, he too could be justified in the sight of God. The lesson is that salvation and damnation do not reside in material poverty or material surfeit. Rather, beyond the material riches or otherwise, there is the critical issue of humbling oneself before God.

Whatever else the parable may say, the story of the tax-collector teaches the lesson that moral regeneration comes when one senses one's inadequacy (Luke 18:13, cf. Luke 15:17). A sense of inadequacy is a sense of one's emptiness. It is the symptom of sensitivity to the presence of the holy God. That emptiness is symptomatic of a sense of awe before the holy God. "Woe is me... I live in the midst of a people of unclean lips" (Isa. 6:5).

That is in turn a starting point for the pilgrimage of spirituality, caring for bread for the neighbour. The rich man who can be brought to a sense of emptiness can have salvation. And this is also the story of Zacchaeus. Materially rich the publican may have been; but in the presence of the holy God, he was enabled to see his spiritual bankruptcy and seek the grace of God. "O

God, have mercy on me, sinner that I am" (Luke 18:13). He abased himself before God and thus became "poor in spirit". May we not draw the conclusion that if the rich can be led to see their spiritual bankruptcy there can be hope for them? The question for me becomes how one communicates with the rich in such a way as to lead them to humility and to the fruits of humility.

Zacchaeus

The story of Zacchaeus is equally instructive. Zacchaeus's name derives from the Hebrew root which means "pure" and righteous. Here is the irony: the man whose name is "pure" is by the standards of the world anything but pure because he belongs to the class of sinners called tax-collectors, the despised scum of the earth, the cheats and bullies. He was rich but most of it must have been ill-gotten gain from his operations as superintendent of taxes in Jericho, the important trade gateway of Judea. Zacchaeus must have had ample opportunity to make money. The text makes it clear that Zacchaeus had made it good in material terms.

The rich Zacchaeus, however, had a sense of emptiness. For one reason or other, Zacchaeus was anxious to catch a good view of Jesus, as is evidenced by his running ahead to climb a fig-mulberry tree. Of course taking a vantage point when celebrities pass by is quite normal. But for a rich man to do this is not quite the thing; it is not in keeping with dignity. So I would like to believe that Jesus had sufficiently registered something on Zacchaeus. Why else is he so curious to see him? The Spirit of God was already at work in him.

The surmise receives further confirmation in the fact that he quickly climbed down once Jesus called him (Luke 19:6) and also gladly welcomed Jesus. His heart had already been touched by the Spirit of God. Of course, the fact that Jesus took note of this despised tax collector is itself an act of kindness, and it could well lead to a change of heart on Zacchaeus's part.

The response of Zacchaeus to Jesus' call is equally revealing: "I give half my possessions to charity, here and now" (Luke 19:8). It represents a vow and a commitment. It presupposes a deep sense of his inadequacy and spiritual immaturity. Beyond that he sees clearly that his possessions had been a heavy burden which was causing him to sink. He further sees clearly that in order to arrest the sinking process, he had to jettison some of the heavy baggage. As a changed person, he has jubilant trust in divine forgiveness and can no longer be a slave to his wealth. But it was no aimless jettisoning of his possessions; he was giving to charity (Luke 19:8). In our contemporary world charity often has a condescending and impersonal ring about it. But in the Jewish context it symbolized sharing in community. By that gesture Lazarus was attempting to share his humanity in the community of human beings each and every one of whom bore the image and likeness of God and therefore was to be his active concern.

The Apocryphal book of Tobit has some incisive statements on the concern for the less fortunate:

> Give alms from what you possess and never give with a grudging eye. Do not turn your face away from any poor man, and God will not turn always his face from you. Let your almsgiving match your means. If you have little, do not be ashamed to give the little you can afford. You will be laying up a sound insurance against the day of adversity. Almsgiving saves the giver from death and keeps him from going down into darkness. All who give alms are making an offering acceptable to the Most High (4:7-10, cf. 4:16).

The kingdom of God is real when we are confronted with the poor, the sick, the imprisoned and the naked, and we respond. In responding to and coming to the aid of the less fortunate of the human community, one acquires "a goodly treasure against the day of adversity".

It is also interesting that Lazarus's response was immediate, and spontaneous. He is giving *here and now*. What a contrast with the rich young ruler who was so reluctant to part with his riches! What a contrast with the spirit expressed in St Augustine's famous prayer, "Give me continence, O Lord, but not yet." Until one desires salvation now, it is a lost cause. Until one has been liberated from the cargo of riches, one cannot expect to get into the safe haven of the kingdom. The call to be poor, like the call to be poor in spirit, is a call that demands immediate response.

There is a further interesting point: "If I have cheated anyone, I am ready to repay him four times over" (Luke 19:8). Salvation begins with repentance of one's misdeeds against humanity. But repentance can be a kind of inverted pride and vanity. Let repentance not be confessing to the wildest dreams. Let it be an awareness that one has fallen short of a definite mark of humanity. Zacchaeus was attempting such a return by declaring to restore things fourfold to those whom he had ever cheated. Reparation, amendment of life and a dedicated life as well as resolve not to repeat earlier mistakes are a part of this repentance. How all human beings need to hear, respond and address this point! How nations need to do the same! As long as nations, while preaching seemingly respectable economic ideas, continue to exploit and impoverish nations, the repentant Zacchaeus had made no impact. As long as any African politician, in the name of freedom and justice, exploits and marginalizes his own nationals, the lesson has not been learnt from the story of Zacchaeus.

The situation in the world today is like the huge elephant dancing in a small room and shouting "freedom" in the midst of frightened chicken running about. Obviously the chicken stand no chance and will be trampled under foot. The nations of the North, like the powerful politicians and the rich in African societies, are today's elephants who are dancing in the midst of scared chicken, the small nations, the poor of the earth.

Today it is recognized that the countries of the North became relatively rich partly at least by the exploitation of the countries of the South. For some time now we have been talking of a just economic international order and we do not seem to have gone far. The countries of the South get poorer while the countries of the North get richer and there appears no way of bridging the gap. There does not appear to be the will to do the right things to achieve the just international economic order. We seem to be praying: "Give us a just international economic order, but not yet."

It is not just a question of giving back some of one's gains, whether ill-gotten or otherwise. It is a twofold issue. First, to realize one's humanity. As long as there are pockets of abject poverty on the face of the earth at this time when we have technological and other material resources to correct the situation, our humanity is at stake. Second, it is an issue of what the example of Christ means for those of us who claim to be Christian: "You know how generous our Lord Jesus Christ has been: he was rich, yet for your sake he became poor, so that through his poverty you might become rich" (2 Cor. 8:9). What does it mean in this context to be as perfect as your heavenly Father?

What has been said of poverty vis-à-vis North-South relationships can be said also of relationships within our respective societies. The story of Zacchaeus is the story of the rich Christian's pilgrimage into the kingdom of God. He is first awakened to his inadequacy and moral bankruptcy despite the heavy cargo of wealth. Then he resolves to return to God in repentance, assured of divine forgiveness. He adopts the attitude of trust in God rather than in riches, and earnestly longs to obtain total righteousness. But he realizes it to be a misunderstanding to hold cerebrally a doctrine of Christ becoming poor for our sake, making no attempt to live it. Praxis and doctrine regarding reciprocal relationship can bring salvation to even the rich man who hears the call of Christ.

The attitude of trust in God goes with humility on which we must comment, if for no other reason than that there is a considerable misunderstanding of that word. Humility is not to be confused with a lack of principle. Humility is not to be confused with cowardice. It does not mean allowing oneself to be used as a doormat to be walked over with impunity. There are three elements in humility. First is the ability to accept correction with grace. The United States of America under President Ronald Reagan has declared that its aid would go only to those who do not criticize its policies. The aid has become the big stick to be used against the poor countries that dare criticize the USA, as for example Zimbabwe which had criticized America's policy in Southern Africa vis-à-vis Namibia, whose independence was being tied to the departure of Cuban troops from Angola. Any nation that would rather wield the big stick than listen to the questionings of the less powerful has not learnt the first lesson in humility.

Second, a truly humble person is haunted by a perpetual sense of failure and is free from illusions. In Afghanistan a foreign power teams up with a local clique to suppress a people's desire for freedom and there is enormous carnage on all sides. In Nicaragua a foreign power is attempting to decide for a sovereign nation not only what friends they should have but also what type of government a sovereign people should have. The assumption of both foreign powers is that theirs is the only system to be followed. That is an illusion, and it is totally insensitive to the failings in their own systems. The painful thing is that in these illusions they use their might and wealth to disrupt and subvert the economies of these smaller, poor countries. There is the implied illusion that by attacking a so-called leftist government, if that is the right description, they are defending Christian civilization. That is one of the heresies of our time. But beyond calling it a heresy, it offers us a common and classic example of arrogance, the opposite of humility. To be humble is to be free from illusions and to be haunted by a perpetual sense of failure, a sense that one's goodness is not good enough.

The third element in humility is generosity of judgment. By that one means that one will make excuses for all others but oneself. In Africa our leaders do things that amount to mismanaging our economies and we blame our exploitation on the imperialists, the neo-colonialists and what you will. This is a type of arrogance. In South Africa every act of violence is blamed on blacks stigmatized as communists. What is never faced is that apartheid, which denies humanity to blacks and others, is a violent system and therefore the blacks are in response trying to gain their human dignity. The apartheid government lacks the humility to see that the wealth and riches of the whites, often acquired at the expense of the blacks, are part of the problem.

What do we make of all this? First, material poverty is not a good thing; it should not be idealized because it can be dehumanizing. But second, the rich can be guilty of not living with the sense of community which God wishes of us. Some of the wealth of the rich can be ill-gotten gain, whether they are conscious of it or not. Some become rich at the expense of others in part because of seemingly respectable, legal but warped international and national systems.

Be that as it may, no one may be outright beyond the pale. But there are conditions which must be met by the rich if they are to be saved. Among the conditions are contrition, penitence and humility. Contrition means a deep sense of sin which makes one completely penitent, so that one will foresake pride, insensitivity to the poor. Penitence does not mean just feeling sorry; it also means not repeating the old faults as well as taking steps to correct the evils committed. And humility means becoming poor in the sight of God. So the rich who sincerely and seriously do something about the plight of the poor and seek to live in community with them also in God's mercy hear the gracious words: "Today, salvation has come to this house".

5. Africa! Where are You in this Blessing?

In the second chapter we attempted an exegesis of the biblical statement "Blessed are you who are poor" (Luke), which is further interpreted in Matthew as "Blessed are the poor in spirit". There we came to the conclusion that the beatitude speaks of two categories of people. First, those who are materially poor, and second, those who are spiritually poor not in the sense of being great sinners but in the sense of knowing their inadequacies before God and therefore humbling themselves under the mighty hand of God and striving to live the values of the kingdom of God. That is, they are merciful and gentle, they thirst and hunger after righteousness; they are pure in heart and work for peace...

The materially poor take diverse forms: the beggars, those who have no one to provide for them like the widows and orphans, those who have no way of earning a living, unskilled day-labourers, the peasants, the slaves. They are the thirsty and the hungry. They are whose who suffer, persons who have no prestige and honour. In biblical times the significant characteristic of such persons was not so much destitution and starvation; it was rather their shame, the disgrace and humiliation that come from being so dependent on others. "In the Middle East, prestige and honour are more important than food or life itself. Money, power and learning give a man prestige and status because they make him relatively independent and enable him to do things for other people. The really poor man who is dependent on others and has no one dependent upon him is at the bottom of the social ladder. He has no prestige and no honour. He is hardly human. His life is meaningless. A westerner today would express this as a loss of human dignity. This is why the word 'poor' can be extended to cover all the oppressed, all those who are dependent upon the mercy of others." [1]

Precisely because of their dependence on the mercy of others that marks them as poor, they become the symbol of the poor in spirit. The poor in spirit is "anyone who is poor at heart or one in spirit with the poor, anyone who hungers and thirsts for justice, anyone who imitates the meekness or lowliness of the poor, anyone who is also sad and depressed, anyone who is

---

[1] Albert Nolan, *Jesus Before Christianity: the Gospel of Liberation*, London, Darton Longman & Todd, 1977, pp.22-23.

persecuted for his faith in Jesus, in fact anyone who is truly virtuous". [2]

The two categories of persons mentioned above are said to be blessed, in other words enjoying God's special and unmerited favour, because they depend on God's mercy. Jesus, so to speak, often if not always, went straight to help them, propelled by a gut reaction of compassion for them, and would lead them into the kingdom of God.

But how does all this relate to Africa, a continent which despite its potential of rich natural resources is counted among the materially poor of the earth?

In focusing on Africa there is no desire to be parochial. Rather, one takes it as a typical example of the fate of the poor everywhere. Of course there are pockets of poverty in the so-called affluent northern hemisphere. A report on the church in the inner city areas of England has demonstrated convincingly that, although people may not be starving like peoples in the southern hemisphere, "many residents in the urban priority areas are deprived of what the rest of society regards as the essential minimum for a decent life". The degree of inequality in society "exceeds the limits that could be thought acceptable by most of their fellow citizens". [3] But poverty in Africa is pervasive and acute. Although there is a small rich elite in every African country, the general run of the people are poor. Everywhere there are signs of the unfulfilled if exaggerated aspirations of the people at independence vis-à-vis decent living standards and security for the future. Large-scale poverty, suffering and degradation mark the continent.

The manifestations of this ugly reality include drought, sickness, corruption, low morale, laziness, malingering and general apathy. They are as much moral issues as they are indices of administrative inadequacies and poverty. They are also contrary to bureaucratic rationality which is essential for the process of development. Bribery and corruption can be indices of an economy that has run off course, a situation in

---

[2] *Ibid.*, pp.45-46.
[3] *Faith in the City: a Call for Action by Church and Nation*, report of the Archbishop of Canterbury's Commission on Urban Priority Areas, London, Church Publishing House, 1985, p.44.

which goods are limited on the market. The most painful illustration of this poverty is the story of the "in-between people" — the refugees and the displaced persons. That story is one of cultural dislocation, homelessness, joblessness and hopelessness.

These indices of poverty are as much the result of Africa being assimilated to the North, being treated as the "backyard" of the nations of the North, as self-inflicted through bad planning and ruthless power-drunk African leaders who have no qualms in "raping" their own people. Abuses of human dignity are much in evidence everywhere in Africa. Poverty and marginalization then are experienced at the gut level.

It is possible to broach this subject of Africa's material poverty from a number of perspectives — economic, sociological and psychological. Here, however, we propose to reflect theologically and religiously on the subject of material poverty. And I reflect as an African. Indeed, I am an African, and a Christian as an African. This is important because it determines my starting point in an interpretation of scripture:

"Blessed are the poor," says holy writ. Does it mean that Africans should stay with their poverty and be resigned to their fate? After what has been said earlier on the story of the rich young ruler, we cannot but affirm the consistency of the theme of God's preferential option for the poor with biblical teaching. But after our comments on the story of Zacchaeus we are obliged also to argue that the preferential option for the poor cannot be interpreted in any exclusive sense; it is not an excluding option.

To talk of God's preferential option for the poor does not mean doing nothing about poverty. The World Council of Churches, which has been associated with the preferential option for the poor, has been working hard with other agencies on the plight of the poor. Its refugee and migration service, for example, in cooperation with the All Africa Conference of Churches, attends to the needs of some five to ten million refugees in varied categories. Its Africa Desk has helped to transfer resources form the North to Africa which in 1985 went into millions.

Material poverty can indeed be a negation of life. Poverty can and does dehumanize the poor. The Brazilian theologian Jaci

Maraschin has written some words which are applicable to the African situation — and to all situations of poverty:

It is no life, no life at all, that's rooted in deception
It is no life when human warmth is missing from perception —
Living is a whole lot more than scrambling for survival
Going through the motions with your neighbour as a rival.

Jesus Christ, he is the life, he is the life of the world.
It is no life, no life at all, in slavery to suffer
With no shelter or voice or money for a buffer,
Living ought to be more like a wonderful adventure.

It's no life, no life at all, when there's no future showing
Mem'ry is not enough to keep a person going
Living cannot be reliving of the past, discouraged,
Life must be attainable and real for hope to flourish.

Poverty, which makes for misery, is not something to be idealized and idolized because it is dehumanizing.

The subject of poverty is ultimately a matter of one's expectations in life vis-à-vis the good life and human dignity. And people's expectations are related to their respective contexts, cultural as well as socio-political. How does Africa perceive wellbeing? Of course, it is difficult to generalize for all of Africa. But the Akan of Ghana can illustrate an African expectation vis-à-vis blessedness.

Among the Akan the key term is *ahoto* which literally means rest and peace of the self. It means wellbeing which speaks of rest, peace and contentment both within oneself and in harmony with the world outside oneself. The indices of this wellbeing are known as the seven blessings: *nkwa* or long life, vitality, good health, felicity and prosperity; *adom* or the favour of the spirit world on whom the living are supposed to depend for their wellbeing; *asomdwee* or peace of mind and peace in society, freedom from perturbation; *abawotum* or the power to procreate, sexual potency and fertility through which the continuity, security and wellbeing of the individual and the clan are ensured; *anihutum* or good eyesight; *asotatum* or good hearing power; *amandoree* or the prosperity, vitality and greatness of the clan and tribe.

In the light of these, the Akan understanding of wellbeing or blessedness is very complex, at once material and spiritual, internal and external, human and non-human, individual as well as communitarian. The highest good is what is best for the happiness of the individual and the community, makes for the survival, continuance and good reputation of the individual, the family and the clan. The biblical message that "blessed are the poor" cannot be experienced as good news until this traditional African understanding of blessedness is engaged.

It will be noticed that the last of the indices of blessedness according to the traditional view emphasizes the community. Blessedness is enjoyed as a community or by a person in community. Here we reach the heart of the African's self-understanding. The African says: "I have blood relationships; therefore I am." To be is to belong and live in a kinship group. A person's individuality is affirmed and fulfilled only in relation to the good of others in the kin group. Interaction, interdependence and bearing one another's burdens become the marks of this sense of community. The sense of community demands recognition by word and deed of one another as persons. It is in such nexus of relationships that the beatitude "blessed are the poor (in spirit)" comes into its own. Practically it means the humility to see Christ in the other person. It means the poor in our midst become living signs of what is lacking in community-building and of what needs to be done. The beatitude "Blessed are the poor" then becomes an invitation to live in community, a community in which if one suffers, the rest suffer. Thanks be to God who uses the poor and the weak to teach the mighty that it is God's will that all live in community.

There is yet another dimension with regard to the understanding of the poor. In addition to the materially poor, there are also those whose human dignity has been denied them, which has resulted in tremendous suffering. In traditional African societies, to be human is to be able to express one's thoughts, emotions, want and weal; in short, it is unhindered self-expression through worship, art and speech. That possibility of self-expression comes of belonging to a community. To be human is to be a social being, and to be able to express oneself as a social being is to have dignity. The cardinal sin of dictators and other oppressors in Africa as elsewhere is their playing God, considering themselves as the fountain and the origin of all wisdom and knowledge and in the process denying others their freedom of self-expression.

By contrast the oppressed learn to rely on God for their survival, thus exhibiting the character required of those pressing into the kingdom. That reliance on God is a matter of faith which has been likened to falling from a cliff and knowing that one is going to land on one's feet because one is never alone if one has faith. It is the quality that enables Africans, despite unbearable poverty, to soldier on and often cheerfully too. It is this quality of faith that has borne witness to the good news of the kingdom and won over many in Africa to the gospel, so much so that Christianity is growing steadily in Africa. One South African church leader in a jocular mood said: "The white man brought the gospel to Africa. He has the land but we blacks have the Bible and the Gospel." This contains a gem: that the experience of oppression and poverty has taught the "blacks" that:

> All my hope in God is founded;
> he doth still my trust renew,
> me through change and chance he guideth,
> only good and only true. God unknown,
> he alone calls my heart to be his own.[4]

Blessed be God who uses poverty, oppression and marginalization to engender deepened faith in both the victims and others.

In relating faith and hope to suffering I know I risk the charge of accepting the Marxist analysis that "religion is the cry of the oppressed creature, the comfort of a heartless world, it is like the spirit of a spiritless condition. It is the opium if the people."[5] This makes religion a kind of perverted world consciousness. Of course, as a later development, Marxists declared religion to be the opium for (not as in the original, *of*) the people. The development makes religion an instrument to be manipulated by others.

The African politician Kwame Nkrumah wrote in his *Consciencism*: "The impotence of the exploited classes in their struggles with the exploiters as the savage in his struggles with nature engenders faith in gods, demons and prodigies."[6] Those

---

[4] Robert Seymour Bridges' Hymn, Church Hymn, No. 665, 1982.
[5] *Die Frühschriften, Marx-Engels*, Stuttgart, S. Landshut, 1953, p.208.
[6] London, 1964, p.13.

who would preach that poverty in Africa should be accepted as a passport to heaven succeed only in falling into the trap of the Marxists of today who would say religion is "opium for the people".

However, the analysis of Marx may not be ignored by religious people. Indeed, the way in which Marx develops his arguments shows some parallels with biblical thinking. Marx, for example, argues the power of capital over the worker and its dehumanizing consequences for human life. This idea of the hostile role of money seems to echo the biblical teaching regarding the enslaving power of Mammon. "Above all it is in the statement that the original power of alienation lies in the power of Mammon that the relation to the biblical perspective becomes clearest. That the power of money can corrupt and alienate man in a peculiarly dangerous way is clearly biblical. It's no accident that in the wellknown words of Jesus, Mammon is styled a kind of anti-God." [7]

Whatever the disagreements between Marxists and Christians, there is agreement on one thing, namely the dangerous way in which money can and does corrupt and alienate people. Read in that light, one may dare to suggest that not to be loaded with money is a blessing in the sense that it takes away some of the dangers attendant on it. This is of course not to say that the poor are saints; there are dangers also in poverty.

The stories of the poor in Africa and the world become the means to shock, conscientize and change people from their self-centredness and cocooned world to begin to see and feel the world from the perspective of poor peoples and beckon them to live in community. In the stories of and about the oppressed, the suffering and the underdogs, we begin to make sense of the gospel proclamation of the blessedness on the poor. And when we understand the gospel, we ask: "What then shall we do to have this blessedness too?" Here theology becomes body language, action as well as reflection. Let me once more quote from Jaci Maraschin:

> The mystery of our humanity is precisely this: that is a bodily humanity, living under the conditions of time and space... Our

---

[7] Jan Lochman, *Encountering Marx*, Belfast, Christian Journals Ltd., 1977, p.70.

contemporary world is divided between beautiful, well-nourished and properly cared-for bodies, on the one side, and despised, ugly and repressed bodies, on the other. Does it matter? Should all the bodies look alike? Or, at least, should they have the opportunities of being healthy and handsome? The gospel of Jesus is a gospel directed to the possibility of the new heaven and the earth, with resurrected bodies. Indeed, the gospel is judging actually the differences shown in our bodies in society... We cannot, certainly, go to the heavenly banquet without them, we cannot certainly love as in the Song of Songs, without knowing that they are also loving through the same beautiful experience, we cannot rest on the Sabbath day without their rest, their joy, their renewed and humanized bodies. [8]

Blessed be God who uses the circumstances of the poor, Africans and others, to teach us the deeper meaning of the gospel that blessed are the poor.

This brings us back to the community emphasis we made when dealing with the Akan expectations vis-à-vis life.

Full blessedness is enjoyed in community. Community is marked by a sense and life of sharing with others in a common purpose and putting oneself out for others. Sacrifices are a price to pay for building community and the antidote for rank individualism and covetousness. That is why one African nation after another opts for one or another type of the welfare state — which is a way of saying that the rich should share the bread and so share the blessing. Lesslie Newbigin commenting on "Blessed are the poor" writes:

Human beings were not made for affluence but God. The poor are not given to us as those who have to be encouraged to join us in the race after futility. They are surely given to us to remind us that we are off the track, that we are lost. It is we, the affluent, who are in desperate need. We have been seduced by the ideology of the Enlightenment into the vain pursuit of happiness as the goal of human life, rather than the reign of God, and we are reminded by the poor that we have lost the way. We are in a wasteland, a desert where we are ceaselessly summoned by all the apparatus of capitalism to go on chasing a mirage. [9]

---

[8] "Theology, Bodies and People", in *Ministerial Formation*, No. 31, September 1985, pp.36-38.
[9] *The Welfare State: a Christian Perspective*, Oxford, Oxford Institute for Church and Society, 1985, p.14.

Thanks be to God that the poverty of Africa becomes God's way of reminding the world of the mirage of affluence. Africa's poverty becomes a call for the search for a just, sustainable and participatory world in which the rich share with others.

That God uses the plight of the poor, as illustrated by Africa, to teach the need for living in community also is a call for a new way forward. In practical terms it means religious people helping to find a new economic, industrial and commercial order that matches, if not flows out of, the Christian perception of human nature and destiny. Economics, the science concerned with the basic problem of choice in the allocation of scarce resources, is of limited value because choice involves value judgments. Welfare or wellbeing involves wider political, philosophical and theological considerations. Economics must involve legal structures as well as communal values.

This theological reflection on the blessedness of poverty will be incomplete without some reference to the church, if for no other reason than that the church is supposed to be the conscience of society. That claim no longer goes unchallenged because many an African political party also claims to be the conscience of society. So it is now a real issue as to where the conscience of society resides — in the church or in the political party in government? The thing that needs to be said is that for the churches' claim to be credible, the church itself must be credible. It is a truism that African churches have become carbon copies of the churches of the North which themselves were built on the basis of the idea of Christendom. That model makes for grandeur, grandioseness, well-fortified edifices like the huge cathedrals, church vestments and vessels of gold and silver. The churches, like their functionaries, are eager to acquire riches. The clergy, by their training and attire, are at the very least middle-class persons. What we have is the model of the Solomonic temple. That model transplanted to Africa, which is by and large poor, not only lacks relevance but also queers the pitch for the churches. Can a rich church announce with credibility: "Blessed are you who are poor"? Perhaps the model for the churches in Africa should be that of Abraham's tent, and the ministers need to be ministers in the tent of a pilgrim people of God seeking the kingdom of God. It should be the tent which goes ahead of the people in the vanguard of resisting injustices that dehumanize people and undermine human dignity. Here we return to the church incarnating the preferential option for the poor.

The issue of poverty is of course linked with issues of power. Wealth goes with power. Many African politicians are notoriously exploiters of their own people; they misuse power. Sometimes this tendency to misuse power is justified as expediency, on the excuse that it is an attempt to build new networks out of congeries of loosely-knit tribes or that it derives from traditional concepts of power. There is enough evidence to the contrary that the person of power, like the tribal chief, is responsible to the people and that a chief's power is dependent on the recognition the subjects accord him. Indeed, power was seen in African countries in terms of the good of the subjects. As the Akan of Ghana put it, a genuine person of power does not ruin the state of which he is head; his role is to seek the welfare and peace of the people. [10] The person who wields money power or political power then forfeits his/her right to authority if they so conduct the business of the community as to pauperize people. What then do the poor do?

Two lines emerge in the African context. On the one hand, the Akan insist that the person of power and influence maintains his/her dignity only by self-respect. So the issue is how to help the powerful to gain their self-respect and dignity. That is the issue in the Republic of South Africa or Ghana, the USA or Great Britain: how can the people of influence and power like the rich and the politicians be made to recognize the erosion of their dignity? How may they be helped to regain their dignity through understanding that in pauperizing others, they are themselves losing out?

On the other hand, the Akan also say: "If you remain quiet, others will use your knife to dress a snake." In other words, those who are not in positions of power and influence forfeit their rights if they do not defend them.

This is a call for the poor and the marginalized to take their destiny in hand and work for their rights and dignity. At the very least it involves a revolt of conscience and a refusal to be an

---

[10] See J.S. Pobee, "The Ethics of Power", in *Towards an African Theology*, Nashville, Abingdon, 1979, pp.141-156.

accessory to evil. The form that revolt takes is a delicate matter which needs to be adumbrated with much thought and prayer. Does it include, for example, the use of violence to break the tyranny of those who pauperize others? A bland non-violent approach *can* sometimes lead to becoming an accessory to evil, especially when the democratic processes have been suspended, and there are no peaceful ways of removing the oppressor. This is the dilemma that has faced people of conscience throughout the ages.

But is it possible for the beaten to take their destiny in their own hands? It is difficult. So for me the issue is how all in community may empower the poor, indeed help one another to be truly blessed.

It will be naive to attempt to solve the issue of Africa's poverty in isolation because Africa's poverty is in part the result of the policies and practices of other nations, particularly of the North. So one of the elements in the solution is how in the matter of economics the North and the South can genuinely share the abundant resources of the world in such a manner as will ensure dignity for all. Here there is need for a real conversion experience with regard to some of the practices in the international economic order. For exmple, the trickle-down theory of economics will have to be abandoned because it does not make it possible for the South to get a fair deal. At the local level, uneven development whereby the rural areas are denied basic human and social amenities will have to be replaced by programmes which guarantee even development. It means helping people to be in jobs in which they find self-fulfilment, which after all is part of blessedness.

6. Ite, Missa Est: Go, You are now Sent Out on Your Mission

The time has now come to prepare to come down from the mountain into the world to live and put into practice that vision which we have experienced of this blessedness. I wish to draw the threads together with the traditional formula of dismissal, *Ite, missa est*, i.e. "Go, you are now sent out on your mission." The Roman Church adopted this from the regular formula for disbanding secular assemblies. The point is that our daily work is a kind of liturgy after the liturgy. Our daily lives are meant to be a continuation of the eucharist. What, then, are the insights we have gained from the meditation on the beatitude: "Blessed are you who are poor, for yours is the kingdom of God", and "Blessed are the poor in spirit; for theirs is the kingdom of heaven."

Invitation into the kingdom

First, that is primarily an invitation into the kingdom of God or kingdom of heaven. In other traditions other synonyms of the kingdom are used: eternal life, salvation, redemption, reconciliation, etc. It is in part the situation in which human beings do the will of God with glad submission and, therefore, are in tune with God and one another. Injustice cannot be part of the kingdom of God. Here the question of the disparities between the rich and the poor needs to be tackled. Does God sanction wealth? That question is often answered in the negative, because national and international commerce is marked by exploitation and selfishness. Indeed, sometimes force is used to impose commerce on an unwilling partner. And so, Proudhon's thesis that all property is theft is very much preached as a Christian idea.

But in the Bible, one seems to hear two voices. On the one hand, one hears the Deuteronomic teaching that the righteous prosper, the wicked suffer. We have argued that the book of Job is in part a critique of this theology which considers righteousness and prosperity as synonymous and adversity a synonym of wickedness. On the other hand, Jesus welcomed to his discipleship rich women and men, Mary Magdalene, Joseph of Arimathea and Zacchaeus, for example. We cannot then condemn outright all wealth. The issue is the limits of legitimate business and the limits of legitimate profit. Business tainted by exploitation stands under the judgment of God. But that is not to say that God can never show mercy on the rich. That is for God to decide, and rich and poor alike must depend on divine forgiveness and divine grace. In any case, if exploitative rich persons are sinners, so too are the poor sinners in other ways. God causes his rain to fall on the just and the unjust. The invitation to enter into the kingdom has gone out to the rich and the poor alike.

The basis for the submission to the will of God is the love ethic. Justice flows out of love. It is thus no surprise that in Luke's version the beatitudes and woes are followed by the Law of Love (Luke 6:26-36, cf. Matt. 5:39f.). Love means genuine regard for others. And that regard means an eagerness and readiness to help the other person because helper and helped belong to the Love-society, and to God who is its head. The rule of God is the situation of love which is more an activity than an emotion.

Again, the fullness of blessedness is never wholly realized here; its consummation is yet awaited. As long as we remain human, our acts of love are at best approximations to the love of the kingdom which itself awaits consummation.

Let us stay a little longer with the love ethic. One element of this love is sacrifice. It is easy to have a sentimental and rather superficial view of sacrifice. The average parent makes sacrifices to see his/her children through school. National taxes are paid, which sometimes pinch, in order to enable the state to provide amenities for the less fortunate. These and other actions are selfless and self-sacrificing acts; they are personal, never impersonal. True as it is to say the levels of taxation hurt, yet it is no secret that governments in the name of incentives give concessions to the rich, which become a buffer against real sacrifice. Sacrifice must affect the individual and structural levels. Sacrifice is a conscious suffering which is not meek submission to the will of the evil doer or of evil structures but pitting one's whole soul against the will of the tyrant. The reason for this is to make real the human dignity which God desires for all human beings. The sacrifice of love is a characteristic of the poor who will inherit the kingdom.

I think our churches stand rebuked in this matter. Several churches are in a privileged position. The Church of England is an example. It enjoys the privileges of the Establishment. Being the established religion of England, it is not only associated with the monarchy and the House of Lords, but there has also developed a symbiosis between that church and English political and literary culture and its suffers from a certain accommodation of the powerful and the rich.

With reference to the liturgies of the Church of England, Charles Elliott writes:

> One will find varying degrees of emphasis on prayer for the poor, the weak, the vulnerable. One will find no prayer for the rich, the successful or the aggressive. While there are prayers for the institutions of state — the monarch, parliament, the courts — there are no prayers that so much as hint at the terrible ambiguity of worldly power. On the contrary it is assumed that power is, and will be, used for the "maintenance of religion and godly virtue". The notion that the powers that be are to be confronted, challenged, chased back to a proper appreciation of their nature and purposes is to glimpse a worldview quite alien to any prayer book ever adopted by the Church of England — or for that matter, the Episcopal Church of the USA. [1]

The church has become captive to the upper- and middle-class ethos. John Wesley's protest was precisely over this failure of the Church of England to relate meaningfully to the workers.

Similarly, the Roman Catholic Church in a good many countries is privileged and not really able to show empathy with the plight of the marginalized. By their privileged positions the churches have become accessories to evil. So then churches that are privileged need to learn to make genuine sacrifices so as to be with the poor, to enable them to speak to and together with the poor, and that the poor in return can speak to them and together they can work for the realization of the kingdom of God.

Let us repeat, the kingdom is never really wholly realized here; its consummation is awaited. That is a reminder of our accountability to God. Judgment will begin with the household of faith. A racist church, an oppressive church, a church that is insensitive to the plight of the poor, in whom the challenge of the kingdom of God is thrown at her, is sure to come under the judgment of God. As things stand now, we are far from a realization of the kingdom. The kingdom will be where earthly,

[1] *Praying the Kingdom*, London, Darton, Longman & Todd, 1985, p.27.

ego-dominated values are turned upside down, so that the dispossessed possess; the have-nots have; the powerless achieve their ambitions; the outcasts are invited in. [2] Then the rich stand alongside the poor, the marginalized, the vulnerable. This calls for empathy, friendliness, readiness to share, the poor as persons.

Holistic understanding of blessedness

Second, blessedness is to be seen in holistic terms. It is not something only of the future. Some garbled versions of the evangelical message see blessedness in terms of a spirituality which is almost oblivious to the here and now; it is a vertical ascent to heaven and people are in effect invited to opt out of the world. But the authentic evangelical tradition insists that spirituality has a horizontal dimension expressed in terms of acts of love towards fellow human beings. Thus according to the parable of the sheep and the goats (Matt. 25:31-46) God and Christ confront men and women in fellow human beings in need, such as the sick, the orphans, the naked, those in distress (cf. James 1:27).

The case of the Evangelical Revival is most interesting. The Evangelicals were concerned with convicting the world of sin and inviting people to receive the Spirit. But they were also the very people who sought atonement through good works by teaming up with the humanitarians to fight for the abolition of the slave trade and to assert the humanity of the less fortunate of society. [3] The Evangelical William Wilberforce was also the humanitarian who carried on tirelessly the fight to abolish slavery. Thus the blessedness of the kingdom is like a cross with vertical and horizontal dimensions. Without the one dimension it cannot be true blessedness.

To change images, true blessedness is like two concentric circles comprised of the sacred and the secular. By the secular I understand integrity and order within the comprehensive reach of human beings. By the sacred I understand integrity and order beyond the comprehensive control of men and women, challenging them to perfection. The true engagement of integ-

---

[2] Elliott, *op. cit.*, p.28.
[3] See E.M. Howse, *Saints in Politics*, London, Allen & Unwin, 1971.

rity and order both within and beyond the comprehensive control of human beings is what leads to blessedness.

Our study of Psalm 144:12-15 confirms the holistic understanding of blessedness: it is at once the physical, material, economic, political, social, and religious and spiritual as well.

But who are the poor who are pronounced blessed? I wish to suggest two components:

a) Those who are materially poor or impoverished, i.e. the hungry, the less fortunate of society, the victims of racism, tribalism, sexism, and religious intolerance. They are the powerless, the weak and the vulnerable, who make no claim on anyone, not even on God, and are totally reliant on the mercy of God. But we need to go beyond these categories to see what this sordid plight represents. Such poverty represents the refusal of human beings to live in the community God called them to be in. It cannot be said there is community when in the one world which God created and in which there are enough resources to go round, one group have, the group next door do not have. Such poverty further signifies that one is not exactly human. In South Africa where, in the name of race, blacks are marginalized and forcibly removed from their God-given land and home to poor areas, the whites have ceased to be human because they no longer have an essential human feeling. Poverty is a reminder of the heartlessness in the world and by the same token a call to the rich and powerful to return to their true humanity. It is a denial of our own humanity at home and abroad. In our world today there is so much fanaticism over religion and race that we need to hear the warning against holding others in contempt.

One particular aspect of the significance of poverty I wish to underline. Situations of poverty create populism which, in this case, is born out of peculiarly despairing and bitter experiences. That is the dynamite of fascism as happened in Mussolini's Italy and Hitler's Nazi Germany and for violent explosions. In this case neither the rich nor the poor have peace. In other words, the disruption of society and community that result from poverty should teach people, at least in their own interest, to seek to recreate society so that rich and poor may truly live as a community.

b) Those who are poor in spirit like Zacchaeus who, though rich, had humbled himself under the mighty hand of God; those who have a sense of contrition for their past sins and show humanity. This group is not to be confused with those who are spiritually poor because of their refusal to be human like our racist or tribalist colleague or neighbour. They are those who accept that they are totally dependent on God and have no claims on God, despite their religiosity or wealth, power or prestige.

This study was done originally in the context of a seminar on "Ministry with the Poor". How then does the beatitude "Blessed are you who are poor" guide, shape and set priorities for the ministry of the church? In the history of the church several images have been used of the church. Two descriptions in particular may be mentioned here.

First, the church, whatever else it may be, is the people of God. It is not just the hierarchy, rather it is the whole people of God. That has been an emphasis of the ecumenical debate as is evidenced by *Lumen Gentium, the Dogmatic Constitution on the Church* of the Second Vatican Council, and the World Council of Churches document *Baptism, Eucharist and Ministry*. This has at least two implications for the ministry. (a) Ministry, therefore, belongs to all God's people and not just to the hierarchy. (b) The church as the people of God is a community. To be a community is to live a life that bears out the conviction that we need each other for our wellbeing and to care for each other's wellbeing. To minister in this context is to contribute to the joy of the community (2 Cor. 1:24). Such labour of the community is the proclamation of the message of reconciliation (2 Cor. 5:18ff.); it is the joyful tidings of liberation and of God who is concerned with humankind. The people of God have a responsibility for the poor, to protect and preserve the integrity and dignity of the poor.

They have a responsibility to vote into office the government that will in reality do something about the plight of the poor. They must provide direct support for the poor. A prerequisite is that people individually and severally should be acquainted with the poor and be open to them, and that because the more fortunate would have experienced the presence and love of God in the less fortunate. Such ministry, however, should not be *for* the poor because that tends to include the worst elements of paternalism and maternalism. The task is that of ministry *with* the poor, which involves standing alongside them and helping them to develop their own self-understanding so that they may become the subjects of change.

Another set of images used of the church and very much in ecumenical circles is the description of the church as a sign, instrument and sacrament of the kingdom of God which is marked by love, righteousness-justice, truth and freedom. Of course, the kingdom may include elements of the church, but it is not co-extensive with the church. This means outside the church too there can be signs of the kingdom. The presence of the materially poor in the world becomes an affront to the theme of love and thus a challenge to people to become poor in spirit by showing mercy-love, to pursue righteousness-justice. Here what is at stake is the example of Christ who "though he was rich, yet for your sakes he became poor, so that you through his poverty might become rich" (2 Cor. 8:9). The poverty-wealth predicament carries within it the potential of a deep spirituality, indeed a challenge to be conformed to the image of Christ.

Traditionally ministry has been understood in terms of three key words: prophecy, priesthood and pastorate. Let us briefly look at these.

Ministry is priesthood. For most people priesthood is limited to the few ordained persons and to certain cultic practices. According to the biblical teaching, however, priesthood belongs to all believers. The people of God are a "royal priesthood… that (they) may declare the praises of him who called you out of darkness into his wonderful light" (1 Pet. 2:9). They are called to be "a holy priesthood, offering spiritual sacrifices acceptable to God through Christ" (1 Pet. 2:5). Cultic practices that go with cheating and marginalization of others are unacceptable to God, as Amos, Hosea and Micah consistently proclaimed. Thus the priesthood is about mediating wholeness and healing. In a very divided world, polarized between the North and the South, the rich and the poor, the have and the have-nots, races and tribes, ministry with the poor means the church and every Christian working towards wholeness and healing, and that on sound and genuine bases. The issue of poverty becomes a focal point for showing the wholeness of God's creation, as a world created by the one and same God and a church which is a fellowship-communion in which if one suffers then the whole suffers.

Ministry is a pastorate; it is to tend the flock. John 10 gives a description of the Good Shepherd. Four things may be highlighted here. First, the Good Shepherd knows the sheep and the sheep know the shepherd's voice. In other words, there is communication between them, which is built on and furthers mutual knowledge. The people of God are called to be the church of the poor, a people who communicate with the poor and know and understand the cries of the poor and struggle with them.

Second, the Good Shepherd lays down his life for the flock. He not only protects them but also is ready at any time to make the supreme sacrifice for them. Ministry with the poor must follow this pattern of self-giving. It will involve leading costly onslaughts on the instruments that pauperize people at home and abroad.

This will of course lead to conflicts and controversy. When the Archbishop of Canterbury gave a press conference on the urban priority areas report mentioned earlier, he was attacked by some Tory politicians as a communist. When the World Council of Churches draws attention to the plight of the poor and marginalized it is attacked as communist. These are indeed the inevitable consequences of taking seriously the pastoral ministry of the people of God.

The Good Shepherd goes ahead of the flock. The church should lead the weak to the land of freedom and strength. But the people of God lead in humility and by service. Leadership is not primarily a matter of rank and position; it is a matter of function, a service to the people whom God has entrusted to its care.

The Good Shepherd comes by the gate and not stealthily by the back door. It is a matter of witnessing to the gospel to go to the poor. But caring for them is not a back-door way of turning them into Christians.

The ministry is prophetic. A prophet is not so much a foreteller, i.e. one who predicts what will happen in the future, as one who forth-tells, i.e. interprets contemporary events in the light of the will of God. In practical terms this means that ministry should help unmask the evils and idolatries of society, to convict people of sin and also to help develop adequate canons of public accountability and professional competence and justice and freedom.

Of course, Bonhoeffer is also right in warning against the gloating denunciation of the world as sinful. But that is no rejection of the penetrating analysis by the Bible of the human condition as sinful. That analysis is forcefully illustrated by the institutional frailty of good intentions. Have not the Marxists, like the capitalists, also exploited Africans? Has not the church practised racism, tribalism, sexism, etc. despite its proclamation that in Christ there is neither Greek nor Jew, male nor female, bond nor free?

Finally the prophetic ministry involves giving hope to the weary and to the down-and-out. But that hope is not celestial dope; it is rooted in and accompanied by suffering, sacrifice and action in the here and now.

I wish to submit that the three notes of proclaiming the word of God, mediating wholeness and healing and caring for the sick and needy are still valid elements of ministry today.